To love Jesus in the seemingly small and sometimes painful spaces of your day, when loving Him can feel long and quiet, is battle-scarred love. It's enduring, expansive love. Karen Stott lives even more vibrantly in private the words she shares with you and with me. This is rare.

Sara Hagerty,
author of *Every Bitter Thing Is Sweet*

With the voice of a friend and the encouragement of your biggest cheerleader, Karen Stott invites you to lean in to your heart's longings and live in the fullness of your God-given purpose, even on the days you're tempted to give up! Sharing her own vulnerable journey as a wife, mom, very successful and sometimes-struggling business owner, Karen offers the wisdom of a mentor and practical tools of a life coach. If you want to know how to navigate the winding path of pursuing a purpose filled, intentional life while being fully present in every relationship, responsibility, and role you have, this book is for you!

Renee Swope,
bestselling author of *A Confident Heart*

Imagine you're journeying through this book with a trusted friend as your heart engages these pages. I trust Karen Stott with my own heart and because of that I can confidently trust her with yours... mostly because I know she is trusting all of us to Jesus along the way.

Logan Wolfram,
author of *Curious Faith*

D0110102

Karen is a woman who watches her words, carefully choosing them so they carry the fullest weight when she delivers them with passion. This is the kind of book you'll want to pick up when you're wondering what's next or what else there is for you, or how you're going to make it through this day.

Jess Connolly,
author of *Dance, Stand, Run*

This book is for anyone ready to step into something better. Spirit-filled and convicting, Karen guides and teaches a generation of women to wake up to the life they've been given and pursue it passionately without delay.

Hannah Brencher,
author of *If You Find This Letter*

Karen Stott knows what it takes to truly live an intentional life. You are going to love learning her amazing story, and you will be encouraged by her heart and her wisdom.

Alli Worthington,
author of *Fierce Faith*

An intentional life is the one we all want to live but aren't always sure how to begin. I'm so thankful that Karen leads the way. With writing that is beautifully rich and moving, she invites us into her own story with such warmth, such vulnerability, and such ease that my own heart was opened to receive the profound truths on each page. Karen is a loving guide, unfurling hope and truth that sets a generation of women free and reminding us that we are meant to embrace God's calling on our lives because we are made to embrace Him. This is a book that will be required reading for my own daughters, and one that I will give again and again to women I love.

Kristen Kill,
author of *Finding Selah*

An Intentional Life

KAREN STOTT

HARVEST HOUSE PUBLISHERS
EUGENE, OREGON

Hand-lettered artwork by Jordanne Van Wert. Used by permission.

Cover by Brian Bobel. Cover lettering by Rachel Jacobson. Cover photograph by Karen Stott

Published in association with the literary agency of D.C. Jacobson & Associates LLC, an Author Management Company. www.dcjacobson.com

An Intentional Life

Copyright © 2018 by Karen Stott
Published by Harvest House Publishers
Eugene, Oregon 97408
www.harvesthousepublishers.com

ISBN 978-0-7369-7132-4 (pbk)
ISBN 978-0-7369-7133-1 (eBook)

Library of Congress Cataloging-in-Publication Data
Names: Stott, Karen (Entrepreneur), author.
Title: An intentional life / Karen Stott.
Description: Eugene, Or. : Harvest House Publishers, 2017.
Identifiers: LCCN 2017014016 (print) | LCCN 2017034582 (ebook) | ISBN 9780736971331 (ebook) | ISBN 9780736971324 (pbk.)
Subjects: LCSH: Vocation—Christianity. | Contentment—Religious Aspects—Christianity. | Businesswomen—Religious life. | Christian Women—Religious life.
Classification: LCC BV4740 (ebook) | LCC BV4740 .S84 2017 (print) | DDC 248.4—dc23
LC record available at https://lccn.loc.gov/2017014016

Printed in the United States of America

18 19 20 21 22 23 24 25 / BP-JC / 10 9 8 7 6 5 4 3 2 1

For Isaac
Because you never stopped fighting

Contents

Part 3: Presence

When God
WHISPERS and
WE WALK
absolutely
ANYTHING
is possible

Introduction

Do you ever ache for more?

I know. Me too. And it feels strange to say *this isn't enough* when so much that surrounds me is exactly what I've been praying for. Or the fact that we have so much more available to us than many people around the world do. All of those thoughts make this nagging ache all the more complicated.

Yet this isn't a contentment problem. That's an entirely different battle. This is about heart, about calling.

This is about that angst in your soul that's been nagging you most of your life. Sometimes whispering, sometimes shouting.

It's been there, on repeat, and it creates a lingering, almost haunting dream that I can only describe as the voice and heart of God.

The tugs can come from anything, but they always pull you in the same direction. Toward justice, invention, art, the human body, dance, building things, teaching things, fighting for things.

Whatever it is for you, it's woven deep. And trying to change it or fight it feels like waging war on your own soul. But what can you do about it?

Everywhere I go I hear people asking about *it*. Wanting to discover *it*, and trying to figure out how to find *it*.

This calling. This elusive purpose.

But in watching my own life unfold and observing literally

thousands of others through leading the Pursuit community, I've realized this *it* we are searching for is probably more basic than we even realize. It's never been about the aha moment. The arrival. You don't just wake up one day and realize you've made it.

A calling isn't a destination. It's a lifestyle. It's simply responding to His invitation with one more step of faith, one more surrender, one more yes.

For years I knew that God was asking me to tell my story. I resisted, as I almost always do at first. I told Him that He had the wrong girl and He would have to wait until I was finished with the demanding mothering of littles stage before I ever committed to writing a book. But yet again, God's plans trumped my own. Within six months of telling a friend I would never write a book while I had young children at home, I found myself signing papers and agreeing to do just that.

Just one more invitation from my loving Father.

One more yes from me.

Maybe you find yourself in a similar space today—wanting to move forward with a new career, a dream, a proposed opportunity, a new city, or a possible relationship. Maybe you're a busy mama, juggling several mouths to feed, the never-ending needs of marriage, and all that goes into keeping a home, all while wondering what happened to the girl under all of those roles.

Maybe you don't have a dream yet and wonder if God will ever use you. Or you think you've screwed up too big, or failed too much, or lost too much to keep going.

Maybe the battle you're fighting is seeing Him in the mundane, everyday moments as you wait for Him to answer your thousandth prayer for the same thing.

Maybe you've lost your joy, or your purpose, or your reason to get out of bed every morning, and you just need to know it will all be okay.

But how? What's next? How do you start over or move forward? How do you smile again when things have gone so horribly wrong or your life doesn't reflect what you thought it would by this time in your life?

Friend, you're in the right place. I've been there too. Still am in some cases. And I chose to say yes to writing these pieces of my story with you in mind.

I had massive fears about writing this book and stepping out into a much bigger arena than I'm used to. I didn't really want to share my story or take the cover off of the messy bits.

But, friend, that is based in fear. Fear of what people will think. Fear of failing my family by spending time on this project. Fear of saying something in these pages that will hurt someone, or confuse someone, or make someone write bad things about me. But you know what stops fear in its tracks? You know what casts it out as far as the east from the west?

Love.

In 1 John 4:18, we're told that "perfect love drives out fear." Someone once explained this to me in a way that finally made sense: When you truly love someone, fear vanishes. Your love for them pushes down the fears of what could happen to you in light of the good that could unfold in their lives. And that's what got me here today.

I have such a deep love of helping others live free and purpose-filled lives that my measly fears of stepping out in this way are diminished. And if writing these words and telling my story can be an avenue of help, it's worth every bit.

Consider this your invitation to the life you've always wanted.

Consider this book your love letter. Your field guide. And if needed, your wake-up call to the life you've always wanted. A life where your passions are ignited, purpose fills your every breath and action, and you can rest fully, presently, and joyfully in the abundant life God has for you.

So grab your cold glass of sweet tea or coffee in your favorite mug and take my hand. Let's adventure together and uncover the greatness behind those beautiful eyes of yours. For you hold more power, and wonder, and impact than you even know.

And the world and your legacy are waiting to watch you live your most meaningful, and intentional, life.

Forever in your corner,

Karen

PART 1

Passion

ONE MORE
step of faith
ONE MORE
surrender,
one more
YES

1

It's a Setup

*Living with purpose means wisely choosing and committing
to a few of the best things for the season of life you're in.*

CRYSTAL PAINE

I'm not sure where the lie began or when I bit off on it. As a girl raised in the church my entire life, I should have been better versed in the concepts of Scripture and what God really says about women. But somewhere between the flannelgraphs on Sunday mornings and the Gospel According to Me, my view of what it meant to be a Christian woman got terribly turned around.

My mother worked my entire life. She has her master's degree in education and spent more than 40 years serving the children in our community as an elementary school teacher. Growing up, my brothers and I spent many evenings huddled around the coffee table cutting shapes from giant sheets of laminated plastic for her classroom lessons the following week. We spent summers helping her organize her classroom, and took care of the baby chicks that hatched under incubator lights over spring breaks.

We were so blessed to be able to be very involved in her work, and even more blessed that she shared our schedule so we could have holiday breaks and summers off together.

Before her, my grandmother was an active member of the local BPW—Business and Professional Women's Foundation—in our tiny,

Mayberry-like town. I remember going to meetings with her and watching her volunteer at the festivals downtown wearing her adorable blue vest with yellow pins. Despite the culture of the 1940s, where the primary place for women was within the walls of her home, my grandma worked proudly as a secretary for the school and other local businesses.

What escapes my understanding is how, with such a strong family heritage of working women, my view of this lifestyle became so distorted. Negative even. It pains me to say this because it's so embarrassing, but I started to look at women who worked with pity—and, honestly, a wee bit of disdain.

As my life unfolded, and I observed the women in my life doing their things, and then I became a wife and mother doing my own, my warped perspective put God in a box. And since I had placed Him in a box, I lived in one too. When we take our own limitations and put them on the God who set the planets in orbit, it chains us to a life limited to our own power. Our lack of faith, in turn, hinders the way we see Him and the way He shows up in our lives.

From a young age I remember always and only ever wanting to be a wife and a mom. There were brief blinks in my history where I wanted to be a marine-life trainer, or an interior decorator, or a veterinarian. But in the end, my heart settled on home, and the dreams of building my own when I grew up.

Until one day I woke up right in the middle of this dream I'd forged for myself, and all of a sudden it didn't feel like everything I thought it would. I was 23, four years into a marriage with the man of my dreams. We had just built our first house, and I was holding the most beautiful sight I'd ever seen, our firstborn, Ava.

Everything was perfect. Blissful even. It was all I'd ever dreamed of, and I was aware enough to know that I was blessed enough to be living in it. Yet something inside me still ached, and I found myself longing to find a creative outlet in addition to my new role of motherhood.

I must give pause here to mention that I believe with my whole heart that motherhood is a beautiful and highly purpose-filled mission. Being a stay-at-home mama is the hardest job I've ever done, and the time women spend sowing into their families is priceless and dripping with potential fruit. I've had the blessing of juggling things in this work-at-home circus for almost 13 years now, and I truly, truly love it. I find the family rhythms, mundane tasks, mountaintop victories, and praying through the hard times together to be truly magical.

But for the sake of this story, I want to focus on the area of motherhood that plagued me with guilt and robbed me of so much joy for nearly five years. The lie that doing anything outside the home and caring about anything other than my family was selfish, disrespectful, and even a waste of time. Sadly, the church I called home at the time reinforced those walls and actually helped to build them higher. Instead of celebrating the beauty and possibility of how multifaceted and talented women are, they chose to teach that my *only* calling was to be a mom and a wife. In their eyes, I was to have children, do volunteer work with the church, attend MOPS, have more children, make more dinners, wipe more bums, clean up more toys, and repeat this cycle until I had raised Jesus-loving, obedient young adults who followed the path they'd laid out for them. End of story.

In that church's world, there was no room for freedom, or dreams, or guiding our children into being responsible, mature humans who lived unhindered lives of passion and purpose as they followed God's call and walked in their gifts. They were all about following a specific, predictable path. And for women that meant marriage, children, and ministry within the walls of that specific church.

As time went on, something about this picture didn't sit well in the deep places of my heart. I just couldn't shake it: If that church's teachings were true, what would happen to me when my kids moved out of the house? What did this mean for women who were never able to have children of their own? What about Sarah in the Bible? Did she have no purpose or calling before she had Isaac...in her *nineties*? What about all the dreams I had that weren't specifically tied to motherhood?

I started to feel completely at odds inside. Was I crazy? Selfish? Or worse...unable to hear God?

The more I questioned, the more ostracized I became in my church community. The people I was surrounded with at that time in my life didn't understand my longing for something different, and they would openly criticize me for not being completely fulfilled in my motherly duties. And worse, they would tell me often that I was being rebellious against God's perfect will if I didn't follow a specific path they believed was right for me.

Now, please hear me, dear reader. If we had the privilege of sitting down to share a cup of coffee and, most likely, some berry-laden pastry, you'd see the fullness of my heart pouring out about this subject. I adore my kids. Head-over-heels, I'll-love-you-forever, squeeze-their-cheeks-off obsessed with them. And I truly, *truly* love getting to stay home and raise them. My heart beats for it. Through and through.

But even though I loved my day-in, day-out mama duties, there was still something inside me, something deeper, that wouldn't go away. And trust me, I tried to make it go away by ignoring it and stuffing it down, but it kept coming back up. It was like this deep knowing, almost longing, that God had something else, in addition to mothering, that He had also created me to do.

Eventually these longings, these passions, if you will, led me to open my own business as a photographer. But the more successful I became in my business, the more unsupported and lonely I felt in my church community. The same friends who were there for me in my journey of motherhood disappeared when it came to the other passions of my heart. And I started to feel as though I was living two different lives.

With their words and comments, they continued to build the box around me. Stronger this time. They wanted to keep me normal, to keep me tidy. I was encouraged to follow God, but only in the directions they had laid out for me. And only within the walls of their church. They had convinced me that they could hear God's will for our life better than we could, and for too long, we believed them.

Don't worry, friend, I know this now to be very dangerous territory and completely unhealthy, and we are no longer under this church leadership, but I didn't know any of that back then.

Despite the opposition I was receiving from our church, my wild dreamer heart and stubborn tomboy grit just couldn't bite off on it. I knew there was more to this story. More to *my* story.

And I know there's more to yours too.

I remember struggling with my quiet times back then because I felt so judged, and on the outs with most people. Even God. But a sweet friend of mine encouraged me to start small and press through. She said just a little time in God's Word each day could be life changing.

And it was.

She recommended I commit to reading one chapter of Proverbs a day for a whole month, so I did. As I got to the last day of the challenge and read through the words of Proverbs 31, my entire world changed. This was not the story I'd been told my entire life. How had I never read this before? How come no one told me? Or worse, how could *I* have missed this? What kind of a Christian was I?

The words felt like a lightning bolt of truth, passion, and purpose, sending shockwaves through my soul and igniting my insides. *This is it*, I remember thinking. *This explains everything.*

> She considers a field and buys it;
>> out of her earnings she plants a vineyard.
> She sets about her work vigorously;
>> her arms are strong for her tasks.
>
> She makes linen garments and sells them,
>> and supplies the merchants with sashes.
> She is clothed with strength and dignity;
>> she can laugh at the days to come.
> She speaks with wisdom,
>> and faithful instruction is on her tongue.
> She watches over the affairs of her household
>> and does not eat the bread of idleness.

Her children arise and call her blessed;
her husband also, and he praises her
(Proverbs 31:16-17, 24-28).

I remember staring at the words in disbelief. Jaws open. Eyes trying
to regain focus to read them again. *This has been in the Bible the entire
time?* I thought. Why, then, was I being taught something so different?
In an instant, everything that had been so confusing for so long suddenly made sense. The war I had been fighting within my own soul
was finished.

I kept reading it again and again as the truth of those verses washed
over my heart. "Her children arise and call her blessed; her husband
also." I almost couldn't believe what I was reading. This woman, whom
God made sure to talk about in His Word, obviously loved her family.
She got up early and cooked their food, made their clothes, watched
over them, and instructed them faithfully.

But it was the other part that got me. It was the other part that sent
me into a tailspin of unlearning more than a decade of false beliefs.
This woman was an incredible mother and wife. Scripture makes sure
to depict her as such. But beyond her roles within her home, she was
a savvy, smart, strong, and wise businesswoman. She bought property
and started a vineyard, and she designed and sold clothing, all without the help of modern-day machinery, electricity, or Apple products,
I might add. It makes me tired just thinking of it.

But then...this is where it gets crazy, friend.

But then...she laughed. She was happy. She was without fear. She
was balanced. Everything taken care of. Nothing neglected. And with
all of that going on, her family *still* praised her.

I felt overwhelming peace and brand-new excitement soak into the
deep places of my soul. Ancient words coming alive in my heart thousands of years after they were penned.

As a lover of words, and story, and helping others, I took to sharing
what had just been revealed to me on my blog. I had started my blog

for my photography business—it was an easy way to share the stories of my clients, gain web traffic to get new clients, and showcase my work. But I never considered talking about my personal life on there. It was more of a rotating portfolio updated with new images than anything close to a sharing about my actual life.

But something happened to me that day that I can't explain, and I just *had* to write. I had to share it. As I poured my heart onto the pages of my blog, a strange and unexpected thing happened. My story began to take on its own life.

Apparently my photography clients weren't the only ones reading my blog after all. I watched the comments on my post explode into the most beautiful conversation among women from all across the globe. As I read through the comments, my story came echoing back to me through the lenses of others' lives, and all of us began to realize we weren't as alone as we thought we were.

I never imagined that one post would change the entire course of my life. But that's what can happen when God whispers and we walk. Absolutely anything is possible.

As things like this often go, one thing led to the next, and soon, without meaning to or even realizing what was happening, I had somehow started a ministry for women juggling babes and businesses.

Pursuit seemed like a fitting name, because what brought us together was our pursuit of the callings God had placed on our lives. This was about the pursuit of doing it His way, where our children, and husbands, and other relationships were honored and He was glorified.

There were 17 of us when we started, and within months there were more than 500. My friend Kara asked if she could start a Northern California Pursuit group to connect with women in her area, and just like that, the floodgates opened.

Within the next few years we were hosting sold-out conferences, managing hundreds of groups all over the globe, and providing biblically centered encouragement and practical business help to more than 25,000 Christian entrepreneurial women around the world.

GOD WOOS
US INTO OUR
CALLING
through our
VERY OWN
cries

And it all started because I said yes and stepped out to share my story.

Looking back at how it all unfolded, I'm still baffled. And every time I talk about it, I'm still shocked that God chose a massively introverted tomboy who grew up in a town of 1,500 people to lead a women's ministry where everyone but me seemed to have it together. But that's how amazing God is. He takes the pieces of our stories that seem like setbacks and uses them as the foundation to set others free.

Looking back at the last seven years, I'm beginning to see that Pursuit was birthed more because of God's pursuit of me than mine of Him. As much as I wish that were different, we humans rank rather high on the selfish scale, and I've come to find that His desire to lift the daughters in this generation to a new level of freedom, passion, and influence trumps my pursuit of just about anything.

So I find myself praying that we can be a society of sledgehammers. I want to break the walls that the world, unbiblical religion, and even our own traditional beliefs try to build around God's daughters. I want to shatter the shackles placed on women that hold them back from becoming all God has created them to be.

Many women have been oppressed and made to feel guilty for chasing their dreams and missing out on family time. Or, on the flip side, staying at home and being judged for missing out on the outside world.

It's as though we as women can't win either way. And I want to help change that.

I want to be a launching pad for this generation to rise up and walk boldly into the fullness of the calling God placed on their breathtakingly beautiful heads.

Both in the home and around the globe.

And I want to take as many people with me as I can.

Are you in?

2

Tears

*I always wondered why somebody didn't do something
about that. Then I realized I am somebody.*

ANONYMOUS

Almost everything I find myself doing now was once something I never ever imagined doing. God is like that more often than we think. He woos us into our calling through our very own cries.

Sometimes He brings us to a place of such raw desperation that we can no longer sit silent. We must act. We must do something. Anything. Because it feels that we are forsaking our souls to *not* do something.

But almost without fail, the forward comes after the fall. Sometimes, dare I say every time, we must go through our own hurts before we can really hold any authority.

I think that's why He allows us to walk through things we never would have written in our own life plan. God wants our stories to take a role in our own healing.

Sometimes He allows us to process through and triumph over pain so that we can be someone else's answer to prayer. Think of all of the nonprofits out there. The ministries. The campaigns. They all began because of a burden. A

> Sometimes God allows us to process through and triumph over pain so that we can be someone else's answer to prayer.

problem that somebody had, a need begging to be fixed, a hole needing to be filled. Someone, somewhere, held a hunch that another soul probably shared the same struggle.

And just like that, a company was born. Or a product was made. Or a movement was started. Our tears often tell us which way to go or what to do if we only stop long enough to listen.

Your passion? That thing that echoes through your mind and is constantly drawing you in? Relentlessly? It may not even have a point, or a destination, or any real mission that you can make sense of in the beginning. But still, you can't seem to go against the grain of your own heart and resist it. Whatever *it* may be.

We need to trust that our tears mean something. That God put them there for a reason and is pressing His finger harder and harder on that sweet spot until we wake up and give it the attention He wants it to have.

We need to press into it.

To do something.

Because chances are high that someone out there is waiting for you to step out, to start. To share your story, or come up with a solution, or create a place for them to belong.

Whatever it is you are waiting to step out in.

Remember there are faces, and names, and stories just waiting for you to do that thing. Because when you do, you'll end up being a tangible answer to someone's prayer.

There's SIGNIFICANCE in the SAVORING. There's blessing in the BEING. NO RUSHING, nowhere else to go. JUST stopping To Sit DOWN, Show UP, AND truly ENGAGE with the ones we LOVE.

3

Seeds

*We worry far too much about outcomes instead of
focusing on inputs. We cannot make things grow.
Period. All we can do is plant and water. But if we plant
and water, God promises to give the increase.*

MARK BATTERSON

Gathering for a meal takes me back to all the good places in my heart and reminds me of the person I want to be. These times around the table together seem to feed my soul more than my belly. They always have.

Maybe it's my country roots and the memories of how, growing up, we were one of very few families I knew that ate dinner together every night.

Maybe it's the whipping about and bumping into each other in the kitchen that was too small for all five of us to work together in that made it so special. Or singing with my brothers afterward as we each did our part in the wash-dry-put-away cycle.

Maybe it's the conversations that unfold and the things we learn about each other when we make a point to silence the world and sit face-to-face—the good bits and the ugly ones.

Maybe it's the candlelight and the swirl of yummy smells that fill the air.

Maybe it's one of those things that fills me in my deep places and makes me feel fully alive.

Maybe it's all of them.

The older I've become, the more I've started to unveil the deeper, truer sources of this longing for fellowship around the table. This time of family, of connection, of showing up and loving well is so vital to my happiness that I've realized it's been specifically woven into my being by the hands that formed me. I believe we long for this time to sit and celebrate in togetherness because our Father in heaven created us this way.

We serve a God who passionately loves family, and kinship, and celebration. Based on what I've gathered from Scripture, I imagine the first 30 years of Jesus' life to have been filled with a large focus on family, togetherness, and friendships. According to Luke 3:23, Jesus didn't begin public ministry until the age of 30. It seems to me God intentionally rooted Jesus in love, family, relationship, togetherness, and in just being before calling Him into ministry. So if God put so much emphasis on this area of Jesus' life on earth, why don't we?

Family is the heartbeat of who God is. Why else would He use family terms to describe Jesus and us? Why else would a dinner with His community be the last thing Jesus did on earth before heading to the garden to be arrested? Why would a wedding feast be among the top heavenly priorities as we step into eternity?

I think it's because there's significance in the savoring. A blessing in the being. No rushing, nowhere else to go. Just stopping for a brief piece of our days to show up, sit down, and see into the eyes of the ones we love.

When I think about these things, I can't get over how much God loves us. The King of all kings is even now preparing a seat for His children at His table. What an honor. What an incredible gift for the King to plan such a feast for us.

As I look back, I've realized that in so many ways, the table has made me who I am and helped me find my purpose. I think we all know what it feels like to be welcomed in and to be left out.

At some point in our lives, we've probably all walked onto a bus or into a crowded room, a cafeteria, or a new job and experienced instant fear.

Do I belong here?

Is there really a place for me?

Will I be all alone?

Not belonging is a real and tangible fear. We all want to have a seat at the table. To fit in. To be thought of. To be seen.

I believe that's why God placed a deep burden on my heart to gather people and give them a place of belonging. A place where numbers and followers and successes and failures don't matter—but beautiful hearts, ambiance, and conversations do.

I dream of a day when every person can rest in the security that they matter more than they can even comprehend. And I pray you can comprehend that for your own heart too.

You were created for a purpose greater than you could ever know. There is room enough at the table for you. Not just because there is physical space, but because you, specifically, fill a hole that no one else can. And your presence, you, showing up and taking up that space, is the only way to make it whole again.

That is the kind of world I want and the type of safe haven I work hard at cultivating.

As we were planning the activities for one of our conferences a few years ago, I had this incredible vision of a long white table overlooking the water. It had gold chargers, beautiful flowers, high-back chairs, and a seat for every woman there.

I immediately followed this thought by e-mailing the coordinator at the retreat center and proposing the idea. Because, as we've talked about, the incessant whirling around of an idea seems often to be, in my case, God's invitation into action.

I knew that they had never done this before, and I was sort of asking for a miracle. After all, setting up a near football-field-length table, bringing more than 200 wooden chairs outdoors, and redirecting an entire kitchen staff to transport and set up the food at the bottom of the hillside would be quite a feat.

But something nudged me just to ask.

I couldn't shake the thought that going severely out of my way to prepare a place for women to feel pampered and loved was an investment worth the effort. So I pressed on. I typed out every detail of my vision—complete with a design board I had created with décor photos so they could really get the visual—pressed Send, and waited anxiously.

It wasn't long before I received a reply, and to my surprise, the staff was actually entertaining it. I couldn't believe it. Over the course of the next few months we worked out every detail of what we started to call "The Art of Community Celebration." And the very best part? We didn't tell the conference attendees a thing. The thought of surprising them in such a grand way made me giddy from the inside out. And when I start feeling that way, I know I've somehow uncovered a golden sweet spot of what I was made to do.

I desperately wanted to create a special time of slowing down and coming together that would remind us all of the goodness God has for us. This fast-paced world makes it apparent that we all need a little more of that kind of time in our lives—to pause long enough to watch a sunset, to love well, to linger a bit longer. Time to just *be*—not striving, or longing, or complaining, or competing, or even *doing*. Just being.

Those are the times our souls come fully alive. When we let go long enough to take a deep breath, to belly laugh at a good story, and to soak in the energy that comes from being around amazing people. But all of that is increasingly being lost in our *go, do, hustle, conquer* culture. And since these entrepreneurial women were well acquainted with a life of busy, and pressure, and striving, I wanted to give them permission to embrace and savor the magic as it unfolded without the pressures of performing and doing anything at all.

I hoped—and prayed—that after giving them a little taste, a little glimpse, of the glory held in this kind of intentional community, the women would love it enough to take it home and cultivate it there too.

The pages of the calendar turned, and the night finally came. I slipped into my navy dress with coral flowers, wrapped my hair in a topknot, and made my way down the hill overlooking the water to make the last-minute preparations.

As I straightened chairs and chargers and placed sprigs of eucalyptus as a table runner down the center, I can honestly say that with every place setting and piece of greenery I touched, I felt a little closer to our Father's heart.

I walked up and down the table, setting out glasses, tying napkins, touching the back of each chair, and praying for each person as I went. Each place for someone indescribably special. Someone loved beyond comprehension. I could almost picture Jesus doing the same thing. Walking up and down the wedding feast table, knowing already who would fill each seat, and excitedly waiting to unite with us, to hug us close.

As I made last minute touch-ups and counted down the minutes until the women arrived, I prayed they would feel it. Tangibly. I prayed that as they came around the corner and saw what was set before them, they would get a little glimpse of God's heart for them. And even more so, that they would be overwhelmed by it. I wanted them to know that what He has prepared is incomprehensibly more amazing. I prayed that in the deepest parts of who they were, they would know that at His table, they would always have a place where they truly belong.

As I finished tying bows around napkins, I looked up to see a few hundred women come out from behind the white brick retaining wall. It was the kind of wall you might see in an old European village. Tall, regal, curving with the pathway, with chipping-off white paint revealing the red clay below. As the women rounded the corner, face after face lit up in a beautiful meshing of delight and disbelief highlighted by the glow of the setting sun on their skin.

I heard gasps and whispers, and watched several women grab their own faces in awe. Others let tears escape from their eyes and fall silently down their cheeks. The whispers turned to a hushed silence as they came down the hill and made their way to the table.

I got a chance to talk to many of the women that night, and I cried during almost every conversation.

"I can't even tell you when I last paused to watch a sunset."

"No one has ever done something so extravagant for me, so lavish."

But one woman's comment stopped me in my tracks and became engraved in my soul. With tears streaming down her face, she stopped me and said, "I feel like God did all of this for me. I feel like He is romancing me tonight. Thank you."

I was so stunned I didn't know what to say, but before I could stop the words from jumping out of my mouth, I simply said, "He did. God did it all for you." And I truly believe He may have.

This is what happens when we give roots to the seeds God has planted in our hearts. They are in all of us. Every single one. And they hold the power to change courses, speak life, and truly change a life.

No one is immune to the plans of God. Those seemingly insignificant little inklings that are embedded in your soul were placed there on purpose. And they are anything but insignificant. They are seeds. They hold the capacity of life itself within their hard shells, but require the obedience of the caretaker and the right environment and surroundings to properly nourish them into their full potential.

This dinner. This table. This opportunity to partner with God to romance His daughters was a seed. A seed in the form of an inkling, a nudge, a burning desire.

> Those seemingly insignificant inklings hold the capacity of life itself within their hard shells, but require the obedience of the caretaker and the right environment and surroundings to properly nourish them into their full potential.

HE has so MUCH
He wants to say
to you, if only
you QUIET
YOURSELF
enough to
HEAR IT.

A seed I took, beheld, and decided to water to see what could come of it.

Over the years I've encountered thousands of women and had hundreds of conversations that have all seemed to start with a simple seed. A God idea. And it made me wonder something.

What is your seed?

What is the idea that keeps nagging you, the dream that keeps you up at night?

What is the *"Maybe I should"* that is coming to your mind right now?

Whether it's the urge to write, move, bring justice to a situation, start a nonprofit, learn another language, or bring a meal to your neighbor, it all starts with a seed that holds more possibility and more power than you can comprehend.

And you owe it to yourself, and to the God who planted it there, to pay attention, give it some water, and take the first step toward bringing that seed to life.

4

Connect the Dots

*Often, the answer to our prayer does not come
while we're on our knees but while we're on our feet
serving the Lord and serving those around us.*

DIETER F. UCHTDORF

I'm not used to being a cool kid. Growing up I was often the last one picked for a team during middle school intramurals, and I was most definitely the senior who was failing chemistry for the fourth consecutive time. I wasn't a child scholar or voted the most likely to succeed, but I did have my own accolades to fill up my childhood scrapbooks.

I had a fierce passion for justice and loving the underdog. I was voted most huggable, and I could fill a small safe with competitive swimming medals. But even so, I always felt like the black sheep of our small town.

Labels always confused me, and cliques made me crazy. It seemed my life was one giant contradiction. I was a loner artist, and I was also part of the popular group of girls that paraded themselves around in matching jackets. I was in student council, and I also spent many afternoons in detention. I was a leader with Campus Life, and I skipped more than half of my junior year of school.

Boxes never worked for me. And when conformity was pushed down my throat, the only thing that resulted was depression and more rebellion.

I never realized it back then, but I think something beautifully pro-found resulted from my stubborn adolescent ways. I learned that life and people don't always have to be one way or another. It's completely okay to be *both/and*.

I don't think the God who set the planets in orbit and imagined everything from the peony to the narwhal would want anything less than for each of us to leave our own unique mark on the world.

I can be both the country gal in boots and the executive in heels.

I can be both smitten in love and positively furious at the same man.

I can be lost in the dream of the big picture and caught up in the details.

I think there's something insanely special about those of us who break the mold. The ones who say yes to crazy invitations and follow God into the scary things that don't make much natural sense.

Don't you?

Growing up in rural America, I was surrounded with patterns and small-town "normal." We were a farming community, where activities loosely followed the harvest schedule and hunting season. We had one stoplight for most of my life. I can still remember the grand opening of McDonald's, which was like the president had come to town. I could hear the roar of the Friday-night football crowds and the blare of the announcer from my front yard. I walked the same high school halls as some of my grandparents and knew all of the founding families of our quaint little town. And who am I kidding? Ours was one of them.

Families stayed, new generations took over old farms, and the cycle continued. My mom would often call me up and tell me she had another student who was the child of one of her former students. In these spaces, the *both/and* rears its head again. The same things that can make me feel blissfully nostalgic are the very things that make me want to pull out my own hair.

My friends applied for colleges and mapped out their five- and ten-year plans. But as someone who barely finished high school, borrowing a ton of money just to dump it into a college education I didn't even want hardly seemed like the wisest choice.

So while my friends panicked about SATs, I hid away in the darkroom creating pure magic with baths of chemicals and a red light. As they typed cover letters and résumés, I sat on the oversized rocks by the soccer field and penned strings of syllables together on yellow tablets of paper.

Steve Jobs once said, "You can't connect the dots looking forward; you can only connect them looking backwards. So you have to trust that the dots will somehow connect in the future. You have to trust something—your gut, destiny, life, karma, whatever." For the sake of this narrative, I'm going to rework that last sentence: "You have to trust something—your gut, your inklings, your unquenchable passions, your burdens, your tears. For they may be the very whispers of God."

It's hard to detect when you're in the throes of it, but the things that keep you up at night just might be your life's greatest purpose. Or at the very least, an invitation to help you discover what is. Many of my friends who stressed about SATs and had perfect GPAs have gone on to become incredible executives in major cities around the world. Their teenage inklings to take studying seriously and work hard on their tests led them into what they were made to do.

As a 17-year-old shooting still-life photos of stuffed animals, I certainly didn't foresee a career as a professional photographer, but that's exactly what unfolded years later. Similarly, when I hid away writing poems under the bleachers at school, I never dreamed that writing would be a part of my actual paying job.

At times it feels as though God has invited us to join Him on the great scavenger hunt that is our life. Along the way He's hidden clues in our paths about who we are, what we light up for, and why we are here. Yet it isn't until we are much further along in the journey, having collected quite a few clues, that we are able to start making sense of where He might be going, and what it all might mean.

And yet, the fullness of it will remain a mystery until the day when we will stand with Him in glory to replay it all.

I'm baffled that so many of us spend so much time trying to decode a calling that we might never fully understand this side of heaven. It's all a faith walk. And I think it's a whole lot less complicated than people are making it out to be these days.

All we can really do is go about our business, pick up the clues as they come, read them, notice them, steward them, reflect on them, and then keep following the Holy Spirit's lead until God reveals the next one to us.

It reminds me of a story about one of my favorite Bible guys, Moses.

> One day while Moses was taking care of the sheep and goats of his father-in-law Jethro, the priest of Midian, he led the flock across the desert and came to Sinai, the holy mountain. There the angel of the LORD appeared to him as a flame coming from the middle of a bush...When the LORD saw that Moses was coming closer, he called to him from the middle of the bush and said, "Moses! Moses!" He answered, "Yes, here I am" (Exodus 3:1-4 GNT).

One of the things I love so much about this story is that Moses was in the middle of his daily duties of tending sheep. He wasn't sitting inactive, stressing about what God wanted him to do with his life. He wasn't chasing and striving and trying to do the next big thing or be noticed by those around him. He was simply living his life and being a good steward of what God had given him to take care of in that season. And in the middle of a regular day, while he was doing his everyday tasks, God showed up in the most unexpected way, with a glorious interruption.

The important thing to notice here is that when God spoke, Moses was listening. And he didn't just listen, he engaged in the conversation.

He picked up the clue. He did the next thing.

He was *both/and*.

Moses was both a good steward and open to new adventures.

NONE of US get the life WE EXPECTED, but if we SURRENDER, we can learn to LOVE the LIFE He Gives.

He was afraid and willing to step out.

He was a small-town shepherd and a leader of thousands.

Reading the story all the way to the end in one sitting makes it feel like Moses would be foolish not to go where God said. I mean, obviously everything is going to be okay, and Moses is about to be set up as one of the greatest faith stories in the history of the Bible.

But it isn't that simple. He didn't get to read the story; he had to walk in it. Blindly. Moses didn't know the outcome; he just heard the invitation. And the best part about it? God already had an answer to every excuse and a solution to every problem that Moses would come up with. In the form of his brother, Aaron, and the stick in his hand, Moses had been given everything he needed to succeed at the journey God was setting before him.

The intimacy of this story never escapes me. God, who spoke the world into being and breathed life into our bones, could have gone about this any way He wanted. He could have created armies from nothing and upgraded Moses' clothing to armor and staff to a sword.

But He didn't.

Instead, He shows up in the mundane, ordinary moments of Moses' day and invites him on the adventure of his life. For tools, God asks him to use only what he already has in his hands: his staff. For help, he can turn to someone with whom he already has a relationship: his brother, Aaron.

And I believe that is exactly what He wants to do with you and me. I would bet that Moses never imagined that the same staff he used every day to tend sheep would be the very tool God would use to part literal seas and free an entire nation.

In a similar way, as a 12-year-old obsessed with taking pictures and a high schooler on the newspaper and yearbook staff, it never occurred to me that those would be the very tools God would use to usher me into leading women around the world to new levels of freedom in their faith, families, and businesses.

In both Moses' story and mine, God invaded our day-to-day

routines to lead us into our destinies, using the tools we already held, the training we already had, and the relationships we were already in. He took what we had, asked us to step out in faith, and freed people through our footsteps of obedience.

And if His character and patterns tell us anything, He wants to part waters in people's situations and free people from bondage using the tools and relationships you already have too.

If you're willing to say yes to His invitation.

5

Stay

*Couples who make it aren't the ones who never had a reason
to get divorced; they are simply the ones who decided
early on that their commitment to each other was always
going to be bigger than their differences and flaws.*

DAVE WILLIS

When Isaac and I pledged our lives to each other, I was 19, and he was 21. We both grew up in the same tiny town and were headed to a completely new life 3,000 miles away on an air force base.

We were young. And smitten in love. And there was no way we could comprehend the magnitude of what we were getting into with this new life together across the country from everything we'd ever known.

Last night, as Isaac played with my hair and sweet country melodies filled the quiet night air, I leaned in and whispered, "Babe, we've been together almost half of my life. That's just crazy."

"Crazy awesome," he said back. We lay there and let the truth of those words sink into our souls. *It is crazy awesome*, I thought. In a culture obsessed with upgrades and updates, I wouldn't trade this long-lasting love for any amount of anything. There's something so sacred about the test of time and staying the course.

At my grandpa's memorial, my grandma had some of her favorite quotes she'd collected over the years framed next to the coffee and cookies. I paused long and hard as my eyes made their way over the words and tears began to fill my eyes. Printed simply, on a sheet of bright pink copy paper, were these words:

> The question is asked, "Is there anything more beautiful in life than a boy and a girl clasping clean hands and pure hearts in the path of marriage? Can there be anything more beautiful than young love?" And the answer is given. "Yes, there is a more beautiful thing. It is the spectacle of an old man and an old woman finishing their journey together on that path. Their hands are gnarled, but still clasped; their faces are seamed, but still radiant; their hearts are physically bowed and tired, but still strong with love and devotion for one another. Yes, there is a more beautiful thing than young love. Old love."

It's only a few months from now that Isaac and I will celebrate 17 years of "I dos." It feels like forever and yesterday wrapped in the same breath. And yet with all the roads we've walked and battles we've won, it's a mere glimpse of the deep truths those words hold. For those words written about old love are the secrets kept sacred for the warriors at the end of the battle. The ones tattered by time and frail from one more load of laundry, one more meal shared, and one more act of forgiveness.

It's the intimacy that only time, experience, trust, and endurance know. And I pray with all my might that I too will hold them as my own one day.

Not even two decades in and I can catch Isaac's eyes across the room and laugh with the knowledge of what's behind his grin. It's like a secret code I've only begun solving. One that has taken trials, time, and grace upon sweet grace to begin to decode and drives our children batty with curiosity. These are the treasures that come with endurance. The secret places revealed in hearts opened only by time and tending.

You can't get there quickly, and you'll be scarred deeply along the way, cut to more pieces than your formerly put-together self can dare to imagine. But as you walk through, broken, fragmented, ripped to shreds, you'll pick up pieces along the path you didn't know existed before. Pieces I can only imagine are what that poet spoke of in the beauty of old love.

Along that path you'll find tenacity in your heart and grit in your spirit. You'll learn what it takes to get shoved deep into the muddy things of life and rise up with dirt in your hair and ashes on your face while still shining bright with joy. You'll find that the real strength and biggest freedoms come with shaking the mud off your skin and forgiving the one who forced you into the trenches in the first place.

And most of all, you'll learn that grace wins. Every. Single. Time.

You'll learn that it's the scars that make you stronger, and that each one sings a victory song that will be heard for generations. Like the rings on a tree trunk cut open wide, the lines will be your legacy. It's the stories of losing it all and learning to rise again and again that will live longer than you do. And these tales of wrecked and rising are the prerequisite to truly experiencing the deep places of love.*

I don't know why I walked my entire Christian life without ever making this connection before, but as I find myself midway through my thirty-sixth trip around the sun, it feels as though I've been picked up, turned around, and placed on the other side of things. The way I see things now is different from before.

Less romanticized, more raw. Just the way I like it, if I'm being honest.

This man I love, the one taking up life space, and bed space, and heart space, looks different now. And though his hands look rougher, his eyes are softer, kinder. A depth of grace and understanding floats between us that we never knew existed before. And our capacity for compassion is larger too.

Years ago, but not so long ago I can't still taste it, I almost gave it all away. The enormity of hurt that had lodged itself between us was too much to bear in my own soul. Selfishness, pride, and buried frustrations gave birth to desires of sweet relief. Our years of miscommunication had gone on and had been ignored so long it became deafeningly silent and caused huge gaps in our marriage and wounds on our hearts.

---

* In this chapter I'm describing a rough patch in my marriage. I was tempted to leave, but I knew staying was what I was called to do, and it's been a huge blessing. For some people, staying is not a safe option. If you're in an abusive situation, ask for help.

A new life, a life without him, teased me with convenience, and freedom, and ease. I daydreamed of packing it all up and driving away. Away so far that none of the pain could reach my doorstep. And the possibility that a new beginning would surely be the anecdote that would wipe away my bitter befores.

But as a dreamer, something strange happened when I began to entertain this scenario and play it all out. When I paused long enough to notice the wake of what would be a certain catastrophic blow to all of our hearts, everything changed.

I imagined what that aftermath would bring. I imagined the brokenness. The children's tears. My tears. All of our tears, really. I imagined two households, his and hers bedrooms, and divided Christmases.

The imaginations made my heart break into pieces, and seeing it all play out in my mind's eye stripped it of its allure. I'd seen too many lives play out this way. Too many hearts crushed in the aftermath of hurt and unforgiveness. So, since it was my daydream, I decided to change the story.

And it turns out, changing the story changed absolutely everything.

I pictured driving away and watching him out of my rearview mirror. I imagined the children's faces pressed up against the cold glass windows, fogged up and wet from tears.

And I turned around.

I changed the story in my mind.

With the car barely parked, I ran out of the car and into his arms. And I chose to stay.

Forgiveness and grace became my anthem that day. And Christmases together, with grandchildren underfoot, was the picture I held on to. The pain of all of the hurt was still fresh, and to be honest, I didn't want to cave to forgiveness and open up to the possibility of being hurt again. But there's a richness that comes when life gives you every reason to go and you choose to stay anyway.

It says, I see you. All of you. The beautifully put together and the brutally broken. And I still choose you. I will always choose you. And isn't that what we all want anyway? To be fully seen, fully known, and fully chosen?

It is for me.

It seems that society today isn't used to difficult things. Maybe that's why there are fewer marriages and babies being born percentagewise than there were a century ago. Our quick-fix culture has Band-Aids for everything from hunger to shopping to finding love on the Internet. The sacred journey of *long and slow, waited and fought for* feels lost on this generation. So when life doesn't go as planned, and we find ourselves desolate and depressed, it's easy to fall into the mind-set that we did something wrong, that we are being punished, or that God simply doesn't care about us anymore.

However, all of this fighting and forgiving, shouting and staying has taught me a lot about God in recent years too. It's almost as if this same path I've walked with Isaac has been mirrored with me and my heavenly Father.

It's been common over the last decade for me to want to drive away from God too. The battles lost, the dreams broken, the loved ones buried. It all became too much. Too hard. "Why would a God who loves me take away so much that I love the most?" "Why have I been to more funerals of people under 20 than over it?" "Why would God fill me with a desire, hear thousands of my prayers about that very thing, and then let them go unanswered?" "Why would He ask me to step out in something and then go rogue silent? Where I can't see His provision or even feel I can hear Him anymore?"

For longer than I care to admit, I bit off on the belief that I was the forgotten one. The unloved. The left behind.

The failures I had experienced in my businesses, the ministry I ran, and my relationships created a perfect storm of mistrust in the One who formed me from dust. It didn't seem that my Daddy God was protecting my heart the way that I wanted, or perceived He would, and I almost didn't recover from the grief of it all.

We were created to LOVE WELL. To live as if the HEARTS in our HOMES and our COMMUNITIES really mattered.

I became convinced that my unfavorable circumstances were intimately tied to being forgotten and unworthy of good things. And the lie that I wasn't loved enough to be protected nearly swallowed me whole.

Somehow, in the battlefield of my emotions, I mustered up the courage to stay. I held on to Him anyway. Even though it was just with the very tip of my pinky finger some days. Deep down I *knew* I wasn't forgotten, even if I couldn't convince my heart to feel the same way.

I hung on anyway. I chose to stay anyway. And as I started to examine God's character and study the lives of many men and women of faith in His Word, I discovered I wasn't alone in this feeling of abandonment. Some people who were highly favored in the eyes of the Lord experienced severe "prison years" before they ever entered their promised lands.

The story of Joseph has particularly gripped my heart as I've read through the betrayals and hurts outlined in Genesis. A boy, highly favored by his father, ends up betrayed by his own brothers, sold into slavery, and imprisoned wrongfully for many years. All of this unfolded while he was trying to live upright and honorably.

The Bible never mentions Joseph's sins as a trigger for these consequences and only speaks of how he stewarded his slavery and imprisonment. It is in these years where I can only imagine how Joseph must've felt trapped, isolated, and forsaken. I can't fathom how lonely he must have felt in that prison cell. How confused he must've been by how differently his life looked from the dreams he had as a boy.

But God's time line was different for him. And it's different for us too. It was in these desolate years that God was doing some of His deepest work as He cultivated Joseph's heart and prepared him to carry out His promises.

It's stories like these, and also my own, that have brought to my understanding that we must pass through a process before we can live in the promise. Without suffering, how can we know joy? Without overcoming betrayals, how can we know true forgiveness? If we never have the opportunity to walk away, how could we possibly understand what it means to stay, to fight, to love wholly and truly?

And I've come to think that's the point of all of this heartache. All of these detours, broken dreams, and failures we experience along the way really are gifts. God knows the goodness that comes on the other side of it all. He knows the fullness of experiencing true joy, and true forgiveness, and true love, and what we need to walk through to be able to drink it all in.

He knows that if we just choose to trust Him, if we just choose to stay, we will come to know and understand pieces of Him that are only available through time and tending. And I think we will come to find that those exact treasures we discover in Him are the tools we desperately needed to carry out pieces of our calling.

It's the secrets we uncover through tattered hearts and wrinkled hands that give us the strength to keep clinging to each other through the storms.

If we keep choosing Him, we will get to experience the wonder and magic of this beautiful, priceless, old love.

And we will get to do it with Him.

Reach Out

Yesterday was one of those days where I started to question whether or not I would survive this whole motherhood thing.

As an introvert, constantly being needed by kids, and clients, and friends, and family, all while running several businesses, was wearing me thin. I could feel myself bubbling up to the brink of an unhealthy breakdown. I pictured myself as an old cartoon character turning red all the way up my body, then my neck and face, until I was shaking, with smoke and steam bursting from my ears.

In times like these I have to come face-to-face with the fact that I've clearly neglected my own heart and am hovering dangerously close to a mommy explosion.

I think all of us find ourselves here at some point. Mother or not. Business owner or not. Where the demands of life, and lists, and loved ones take over the care of our own souls and send us barreling into the very worst versions of ourselves.

On this particular day, though, my overwhelm was specifically tied to my need to be alone, and the tiny humans who shared my space didn't understand this deep need of their highly fraud-functional, introvert mama.

Fraud-functional is a word I've made up to define my life most days.

I'm functioning, sure, but barely. Dinner is made, the kids are clothed, kind of, and I'm pretty sure I'm carrying on conversations, or at least answering questions, but I'm not connecting. My heart is a million miles away, retreating into a safe place while my face glazes over and nods at the incessant demands that come with raising a family and running a home.

In this space I stop laughing, or even smiling for that matter. And for me that's a huge, flashing red light that something is severely wrong. Everything feels like a weight, and joy and peace seem nowhere to be found.

I started to feel my insides tremble in frustration and my breathing change, and I realized I had a choice in how this story continued to play out. Would I continue pressing on when burnout, and let's face it, explosive mommy was looming? Would I let the fear of being a burden to someone else rob them of being a blessing instead? Would I insist on doing everything on my own and lose my cool in front of the kids? Or would I realize that I couldn't do this alone, call for help, and give my heart the time it needed?

As a working mama, situations like this used to paralyze me. One of my biggest fears is failing on my responsibilities as a mother and having to ask for help. I have a hard time getting past the fact that the kids are my responsibility, and I don't want to burden someone else with watching them. It took me a long time to realize other people didn't feel burdened by my children, and actually, my letting go and reaching out was a blessing to them too. Thinking my children were a burden for others and solely my responsibility was a lie I had made up in my head and placed on other people that simply held no truth.

So last night, as the smoke of frustration was rising up and clouding my brain, I stopped, and I chose to reach out instead. I asked a friend to come over and stay with the kids for no other reason than to save me from losing my absolute mind.

When my friend got there, I got in the car and drove straight to a nearby lake. I didn't turn on the radio, or a podcast, or anything else to fill my mind and rob me of the silence I so desperately needed. I rolled down the windows and let the wind tangle my hair. I used one hand to drive and the other to surf the breeze out my window.

And it felt like the most needed therapy.

When I arrived I walked around the lake at the slowest pace humanly possible. I breathed in the summer air and watched sailboats glide across the water as high schoolers sat chatting on the shore. I had time to think, and breathe, and pray, and dream. And for the first time in a really long time, I actually felt like me again.

Value can't be placed on time like that. Time to be refreshed from the inside. To be filled up by the very Voice that spoke us into being.

It's priceless. And necessary. And oftentimes, especially for us women, it's one of the first things we say we can do without.

But we can't. We need each other, friend. We just can't do this alone. Even God created in trinity. He paved the way for us to do life in community by being community first. But sometimes we need to get out of our own way, and past our own fears, and let it actually happen. We need to breathe in, let go of the lies we've let in, and allow the people who love us to really love us, tangibly.

Honestly, we need to get over ourselves. We need to be okay with help and realize that our best selves emerge when we admit we can't do everything. Or at least do everything well.

There have been times over the course of our marriage when we've been rich in friendships and community, and there have been times when we celebrated our birthdays all alone. I know what it's like on both sides of the fence, and can I just say that finally finding a group of friends that feels like your own home is worth every awkward effort and uncomfortable invitation you may have to walk through to find?

Early in our marriage, shortly after moving back home to Oregon from Florida, Isaac and I got a bit bummed out because we discovered that some of our friends were hanging out without us. And now that we have so much social media, this is something I'm sure all of us encounter and struggle through at times.

Honestly, WE NEED to get over ourselves. We need to be OKAY WITH HELP & realize that our BEST SELVES emerge when we ADMIT we CAN'T DO everything.

All of the thoughts began to swirl in our minds about how they must not like us anymore, or that we had been replaced, or that maybe we weren't even fun people in the first place. We felt bad for ourselves for a good solid while before it dawned on me: *Well, someone had to invite the other.* I said to my husband, "Someone had to make those plans, and make the calls, and set out to do something. If we want friends like that, then we need to go be friends like that."

With that one revelation, my whole perspective on all of this shifted, and I began to put the weight of cultivating friendships on myself instead of blaming others for not loving me like I wanted. And that shift changed everything in this area.

The friends and community conversation is a difficult one for some, I get that. And if you've been left, burned, betrayed, or lied to, it's all the more difficult to get back in the game. I get that too. Truly I do.

But it's worth fighting for, friend. You can't do this alone. You really can't. So if you are waiting for someone to call or text you, call or text them instead. If you wish someone would invite you out for coffee, be the one to invite someone else out for coffee. If you are all alone on New Year's Eve and you wish you had somewhere to go, or someone to kiss at midnight, plan a party and give everyone, especially you, a fun place to belong.

It's much harder to place the responsibility for how our lives look on ourselves than it is to complain. It's much easier to throw a pity party for one than host a real party for a handful. But the best things in life are very, *very* rarely the easy things, friend. And those things that seem difficult, or hard, or even impossible, pressing through with those things is where we find the gold.

My encouragement to you, dear reader, is to be an invitation to someone else. Chances are extremely high you're not the only one wishing you had someone to hang out with, or a place to go, or a party to attend. So reach out, send that text, make that dinner, plan that thing.

Be the answer to someone else's prayer.

7

12, 3, 1

*Above all else, guard your heart, for
everything you do flows from it.*

PROVERBS 4:23

As I've opened my ears to hear the cries of our culture, I'm struck by the vast sense of isolation and disconnectedness we all seem to be enduring. In a day and age where we can be connected to someone at any second of any day, it feels as though what really matters—the in-person heart-to-hearts and circles of accountability—are dwindling at an alarming pace.

People are constantly talking, but rarely connecting. Everyone feels they have the right to speak into the lives of everyone else, and I'm constantly shocked at the things people say to one another behind the safety of their screens.

Since I highly doubt that you, precious reader, are laying into people online, I want to talk for just a minute about what it's like to be on the other end of this phenomenon and how we can navigate righteously through it.

We can learn so much from Jesus about relationships. As the Son of God, He was called into a life of service, love, and availability—but notice He didn't open His heart to everyone. That, He guarded. He could speak to 5,000, but He came home to 12. And within those 12, there were 3 He was closest to, and out of them, just 1 who was closer than a brother.

Proverbs 4:23 warns us: "Above all else, guard your heart, for every-thing you do flows from it." Jesus was the perfect example of this. Somehow it seems this has gotten out of check lately. We now live in an age where we can speak to 5,000 people at once, but we've simulta-neously opened ourselves up to being judged and spoken to by those same 5,000 voices. When we absorb thousands of comments on the Internet from people we don't even know, we aren't doing a great job of guarding our hearts, are we?

If we give space to every social media criticism or unwanted nega-tive e-mail, we are opening up precious parts of ourselves to be shaped by people who would rather break us down than build us up.

Not everyone should get a voice in your life. Hear me here. This bears repeating. *Not everyone should get a voice in your life.* Since our hearts determine the course of our lives, I think it's time we stand up and fight for them fiercely.

Friend, we would never allow someone to walk into our homes and say the things to us that we allow to fill our hearts when we engage online. In these times we need to stop worrying about what the person on the other end thinks and fight to guard our own hearts. In my life, this has involved hiding people on social media, unfollowing people, and sometimes even unfriending them. It means filtering e-mails so the negativity doesn't make its way into my mind, and then to my heart.

It disturbs me that I even have to write about this topic, but when I'm watching these things destroy the hearts of people I love, I can't *not* say something. As trivial as all of these boundaries sound, I beg you to try some of them and just see if they make a difference in your heart and your perspective.

At one of our Pursuit retreats, I listened as an attendee told one of our speakers she had to unfollow her on social media. Seeing the speaker's happiness in her marriage was too painful for this attendee as she endured heartbreak in her own marriage. It was a lightbulb moment for me as I realized we don't just need to guard ourselves against negative people, hurtful words, or distasteful rants, but also from things that can spurn our own hearts into self-pity, comparison, jealousy, or discontentment.

When we shed the BUSYNESS of UNENDING tasks to study the beauty of our UNIQUE SOULS, we'll find PIECES of our PURPOSE AWAKEN. And glimpses of the FATHER we may have never noticed before.

I was so proud of this gal for admitting her limits, and even prouder that she had taken action to guard her own heart. It's not easy to admit to ourselves that the girl with the perfect house or perfect marriage or eight babies or thriving business thousands of miles away is causing envy and jealousy in our hearts, but this is reality for so many of us.

It's times like these—where we spot the ugly in our own souls—that we must take action to protect what is precious to us...our very heart. If you constantly find yourself getting hung up on a specific person or circumstance that you just can't stop thinking about or bringing up, it might be healthiest for you to put some distance there. If your mind is spinning out of control because of the negative things you're reading and allowing in, maybe you should put up some boundaries and take some steps to not see those things.

And if you find yourself longing to have your own 12, or your own 3, or your own 1, but you've been lost in trying to prove something to the 5,000, maybe it's time to refocus.

Maybe it's time to lay down the voices of the Internet and focus on the relationships with people who are praying for an invitation instead.

Imagine if every one of us reading these words stopped scrolling through others' lives and started sowing into our own. I can almost picture it now. A world full of intentional relationships, uplifting in-person conversations, and full tables.

A world where no one has to celebrate the upcoming birth of their child alone or turn another year older at a table for one.

We were created for connection, woven with the need for invitation and belonging. It's not about building a massive organization, a well-loved brand, or a thriving business. While those are good things, getting it out of balance might be costing us the very best of things.

I'm starting to learn more and more that this whole intentional life I'm trying to cultivate is wrapped up in loving well, one invitation at a time, and living life as if the hearts in our homes and people in our communities are the treasure that matters most of all.

8

Lean In

Every person's life is a fairytale written by God's fingers.

HANS CHRISTIAN ANDERSEN

I always imagined it differently, the best parts of my childhood meshed with the joy and peace that a God-filled marriage brings to a home. It laid out like a fairy tale, with Isaac's blue eyes and my jet-black ringlet-curled babies in my mind.

I pictured a long, tree-lined country driveway full of cherry blooms and a tire swing hanging from the giant oak just west of the front porch. The boys would run there, and a big dog would chase them as the field dust whisked off their boots, meeting the sun as it kissed the horizon.

Isaac and I would watch them and smile. We would hold hands on the steps as the evening rose and the day said good-bye. There would be sun tea, and laughing, and boys jumping dirt bikes as my girl twirled and danced in her floral dresses.

It would be stable and true. A messy mix of sweet country melodies and '90s rap lyrics would rumble through our walls, sometimes at the same time.

It would be cozy, and worn, and perfect. It would be home. And so perfectly us.

But that's not exactly how it has played out.

When I was eight years old, my family sold their fifty-some acres in the woods and moved to the city. (And by city, I mean a bustling metropolis suburb that teetered between 1,000 and 1,500 people.) It was traumatic, to say the least. My brothers and I were used to the freedom, and imagination, and adventure that came with living on our very own Wild West frontier.

We were used to being gone for hours, trudging underneath towering evergreens and wet, dripping moss to build pirate ships on pieces of plywood we'd thrown on the wild blackberry bushes and then eating "food" from the bark of the trees.

When we moved to town, the adventuring slowed and slowed until there was no longer a trace that it had ever existed.

We would still play in the trees in the backyard, but there's something different about exploring when you're surrounded by fences. You can really only go so far.

I remember climbing to the very tiptop of the cedar trees that lined our fence. There, with sappy hands, surrounded by rich-smelling branches 30 feet above the ground, I found something completely magical.

And after a while, without even realizing it, that branch at the tiptop of that cedar out back became my safe place.

I would sit there mesmerized as the sun set over the mountains and I watched the town slowly shut down for the night. It was peaceful there. And I guess it was a small glimpse into my heart too. How I always wanted to see beyond the fences. How my heart couldn't handle being reined in or not being able to say good night to the sun.

I longed for freedom even then. I longed for a life without the restrictions of fences, or boundaries, or the close proximity of neighbors and their invasive noises.

When I grew up, things would be different, I declared to my young self. When I could make decisions on my own, I would choose the ones that allowed me to feel peaceful, and alive, and free again. The ones where I would twirl with my dress and let the field dust dance off of my boots.

AT CERTAIN TIMES, our efforts and GOD'S WILL ALIGN, and things we never thought WOULD AMOUNT TO anything end up changing EVERYTHING.

But being a grown-up is different from what my adolescent self had imagined. It makes me understand Peter Pan a little bit better too. The older I get, and the more life hits me, the more I understand this desire for a place where I don't have to grow up.

A place where I wouldn't have to watch life destroy my dreams. A land where I could make the rules and control the outcome. And maybe fly a little bit too. When you find yourself waking up as a grown person, with the weight of the life that has been handed to you starting to suffocate your soul, Neverland starts to feel a whole lot more inviting.

I remember getting out of the shower one day after having a lengthy chat with God (because that's the best place for conversations like that), and I just wept. I lay on my bed in a blubbering mess of tears. We had 21 days until our house closed and we needed to be boxed up, accounted for, and out of our house.

But we had nowhere to go.

I try really hard to wrap my mind around the Father heart of God in moments like these. And as I reflect on this story now, it seems a bit surfacey compared to some of the faith-hitting-the-wall situations we've walked through in recent years. But for the sake of this narrative, we will just stick to this story.

I feel like a gigantic brat admitting this, but there have been many times in my walk with the Lord, including this one, when I have thought to myself, *I would never treat my kids like this.* Have you ever felt like that when waiting on a prayer? If I was going to churn a dream in my children's hearts, I would most certainly have a plan in my head to help it come to fruition. And I would most definitely keep them filled in along the way so they knew I was taking care of it.

But in this faith journey, I'm learning more and more that God doesn't exactly work like that. And even though I know in my head that He is good, our looming homelessness and years of unanswered prayers made me feel all sorts of forgotten as this event unfolded.

As dramatic as this sounds, at this point I barely had a shred of hope left. And it wasn't only this particular situation pushing me over the edge into a faith crisis. It had just been too long. Too much. Too many unanswered prayers. Too many disappointments. Too many abandonments, betrayals, and broken dreams over the course of the previous seven years.

I was exhausted. And tired of hanging on just one more time. Especially when the answers before weren't what I'd expected or prayed for.

It was just all too much.

I was just done.

Have you ever been there?

This was the summer between our son's second- and third-grade year. He was eight. The same age I was when I moved for the first—and last—time during my childhood. But instead of experiencing his first move, he was on his sixth...in eight years.

I can't even process how far our reality was from the dreams I'd had for my family as a newlywed. Every moving truck brought with it another bucket of tears adding to the river of my continually breaking heart.

Why. Just, why?

It was never supposed to be like this, I thought to myself. We were supposed to have *a* home. Singular. One our children could call theirs and drive by with their children in 30 years, telling them all of the stories from the one backdrop of their childhood. They weren't supposed to have a rabbit trail of memories, and bedrooms, and addresses that held no foundation and gave no structure to their little souls.

It was all just supposed to be so different.

I read a quote once that said, "I think what can mess with our happiness the most is the idea in our heads of what our lives are supposed to look like." And I can't articulate anything that would be more spot-on for me. When what we imagine we will have slams into the reality of what we wake up to day after day, it holds the power to really mess with our hearts. Or even take us out completely if left unchecked.

If you're a dreamer like me, you may have had scrapbooks and notebooks filled with magazine clippings of how you wanted your life to go. Mine always held photos of white barns, fields of grazing horses, and sometimes lakes. I had dreams of renovating an old farmhouse where we brought home all of our babies and tucked them in for their whole lives.

And I imagined we'd do the very same thing when our grandkids came to visit.

I pictured our home full of lifelong friends and family, and imagined how we would host weddings and events by the barn as the sun set.

But none of that has happened. And worse, our dreams have been raked over the coals in the last 12 years. Every preparation, every safeguard, every plan we had made for our family to ensure that we would get the lives we dreamed of has somehow fallen through our fingertips. But honestly, it feels more like they got ripped from my tightly gripped fingers than loosely falling.

From the housing crash in 2008, to perfectly good cars breaking down on the side of the highway, twice in a row, to contracts that weren't upheld, to a flood destroying everything in its path, to having products in our shop stolen and copied, and worst of all, to having people come into our lives with huge promises that turned out to be a series of lies. It felt as if every aspect of our dreams was bait for the enemy to come eat it away.

For years I set up my tent in the camp of resentment and bitterness. I was so angry with God for stripping away the things I wanted most that I couldn't even see that He had filled my life with the things I actually needed most.

And this was very scary, very dangerous ground.

Through everything that had unfolded in our lives, this verse kept popping up in my path, and it started to feel like it was singing a familiar tune.

In their hearts humans plan their course,
but the LORD establishes their steps (Proverbs 16:9).

I had gone my entire life reading this verse wrong. Somehow I had made it up in my head that it actually read, "A man plans his way, and the Lord helps him get there." The fact that we could be doing what's right, tithing, seeking wise counsel, setting up IRAs, and trying to be good stewards of all things, and not end up with the results we had set out to attain was beyond me. I simply didn't understand how in God's economy two plus two didn't always equal four.

Along the way I planned to have four kids, build my dream farm-house, adopt, and have a thriving business and a solid community of friends. We were following God and doing our best to honor Him in everything we did. So in my mind, that should equal life going peachy and things turning out the way that I wanted. Right?

Not so much.

The way it actually unfolded was more like a constant crippling of our dreams and a slammed door to many things we tried to pursue. I started multiple businesses that I thought were great ideas, but they failed miserably. We poured our life into a church, and friendships, and a community that turned out to be a dangerous, twisted web of spiritual abuse. We ate well and lived active lifestyles, and still my body continued to let me down and cause me so much pain I could no longer do the things I used to do.

Turns out, as I should have known, Proverbs is right. I can plan all I want, but it's the Lord who will decide if something is going to go forward or not. And in what season it will or won't be successful.

Over the past 12 years I've started a photography business, a mentoring program, a magazine, a clothing line, a home shop, an international women's ministry, a cross-country workshop tour, a journal company, a kids' devotional line, a conference for creative business women, a dream wedding giveaway community, an educational wellness community, a directory of Christian businesses, an online course for how to start businesses, and I'm pretty sure at one point I was also a Mary Kay lady.

The thing about all of these ventures is that I started them almost all the same way. I built incredible websites, sought out ambassadors to help spread the word, hired an insanely awesome video and photo crew, checked off all of the boxes on running a successful launch, and still, the outcomes of each of the companies couldn't have been more opposite of what I intended them to be.

The clothing company I started was called Ruby Apparel, and I absolutely adored the whole thing. It was years ago. Long before cute Christian shirts were a thing. The website was one of the best ones we had ever designed. We had put together the most insanely beautiful photo and video shoot on the beaches of Santa Barbara with our adorable mock-up tees and tanks to add to the website, and I was smitten.

It was all going incredibly well, until *I* wasn't.

A few weeks before launch I realized I had no desire to run a clothing company with the production option that was currently available to me. I didn't want to deal with inventory, or shipping, or returns of items that didn't fit well. And although it was something that I could do, and really enjoyed pieces of, it wasn't something I felt we were supposed to move forward with. That business never made it to launch day, and looking back I am so, *so* thankful it didn't.

I've also launched other products and businesses that I was super excited about, but when they launched they landed with an absolute thud. No one bought the products, and I kept pouring money into creating new ones, thinking that someday everything would just click and we would somehow make it successful.

Sometimes I got the hint quickly, while other times it took me years to realize my efforts were in vain and the project was obviously something God was closing the doors on.

And then there were things like Pursuit, and our children's quiet time journals, Adventures with Archer, and starting a business with Young Living that seemed to be overflowing with His favor. All of those endeavors were businesses we never even meant to start in the first place. But we stepped out in faith after God's prompting, and they took off like wildfire.

It's things like these that make us feel invincible, and smart, and, let's just face it, the success feels kind of amazing. It's almost as if we have some sort of magic sauce or special secret that makes us so successful.

But the truth is, we didn't do anything special. God did. At certain times, our efforts and God's will align, and things we never thought would amount to anything end up changing everything. I've heard stories like this over, and over, and over, and I think it's time we pay attention to them.

My good friend Elizabeth often says, "Leaning takes trust, but pushing takes effort." Sometimes we start something because we have a little inkling, and we need to trust that God is going to do something with it. Other times we start something because we just want it to work so badly. It's needed in the marketplace, and it's such a great idea, but instead of things flowing effortlessly and seamlessly falling into place, it feels as if we are trying to push a boulder up a mountain. And it turns out, that was never a boulder we were supposed to be pushing in the first place.

Or maybe it was—we just tried to push it at the wrong time or in the wrong season.

That was my farm dream. I had this idea in my head of exactly how my life would play out. I had big plans about what business ventures would work, what our friendships would look like, and how our lives would play out. And when it didn't end up that way, I became a prisoner to my own pity party. What derails our destiny most is coveting what we would rather have for our lives instead of being thankful for what God has given.

In my experience it seems that sometimes God places His hands on the ventures we pour our hearts and time into. Other times He just doesn't. There's no foretelling it, no trying to figure it out before He decides to reveal it. It's just how He seems to be working things in my life. And maybe in yours too.

It's not because of something we do or don't do. Or a way we've failed or succeeded. It's just His divine plan. Playing out the way it needs to so that He can ultimately carry out His very best for our lives. Even when it makes no sense to us.

I have no idea why certain things I've started have failed so misera-bly. And just as startling, why other things succeed beyond my wildest dreams. Sometimes God opens doors, and other times He closes them. And as hard as it can be to come to terms with this, our job is simply to listen, to pay attention, and to follow His leadings.

As painful as this picking-up and laying-down dance has been, along the way I've learned that we will only be able to embrace our fullest calling when we surrender all of our pieces, dreams, and gifts to be used as God pleases. We must be willing to lay down the life we thought we wanted and pick up the one He has for us.

And you know what happens when we do? The dreams we once had for our lives suddenly pale in comparison to the plan He has laid out for us all along. I just couldn't see this when I was holding my own dream so closely. So tightly. It was almost as if my dream for my life was something I worshipped more than I did His face.

But I'm learning now that we've got to listen and pay attention. We need to open our eyes to which doors God is opening in our lives and which ones He's closing. Because, friend, I know wherever He's lead-ing us, it's going to be good. Because that's just who He is.

The life I have now is nothing like I imagined it would be back then. Our kids are spread out unevenly and far apart. We haven't adopted yet. I don't even know if that is something we will ever do, or a dream I must lay down as well. I simply don't know.

We live in a '70s ranch house, which is my least favorite architec-tural style. Our friendship circle is small but deep. And it looks vastly different than I thought it would. I'm doing a job I never, ever thought I would do and actually ran from for nearly a decade.

It all looks alarmingly different from the life I planned out on dream boards with my friends. But once I stopped clenching my fists and banging them against His chest over all of the losses, I started to see that this different life holds beautiful blessings too.

There's something so deeply fulfilling, so joyous, about following God into the scary things He asks of us and setting our preconceived notions aside. It's a sign of bravery, and courage, to drop your hands to your sides and look up to the sky in surrender. Breathing in what He has given, and thanking Him for it. Even if it's not what we would have planned for ourselves.

It's in the following of the One, not in the forging of our own path, that our truest happiness lies, our purpose is found, and the smile on our face returns.

But we must open up our hands, and our hearts, and our dreams, and be willing to let go, lean in, and embrace this life He's planned for us.

So get ready, friend...because when you can finally close the door on what you wanted your life to be like and walk through the door of what God is inviting you into, and the goodness He has for you there, absolutely everything changes.

In a really good way.

9

I Can't Survive

The best way out is always through.

ROBERT FROST

The nurses were buzzing around, telling me to hold it in. "Whatever you do, don't push," they said.

Yet all I could do was close my eyes and try to tune it all out.

My body heaved and shook involuntarily as it took over to bear a miracle. I couldn't stop it or hold it in as they demanded I try. I started to bite the rail of the hospital bed as my formerly sane self bombarded my mind. *Biting the rail? Are you serious? This is disgusting. What barbarian would do such a thing? Don't you know how appalling this is? And how germ infested? Gross.*

I could feel my body tense up in pain and rise off the table as I death-gripped the hard, plastic bed rail. And then, in a moment of pure glory, my body released me back to the table like a puddle of Jell-O for a brief glimpse of sweet relief.

"I can't do it," I said. "I just can't." The pain had become one constant contraction, and I pleaded with God to pull me out of my own skin. As I begged someone to bring me drugs, my friend Tiffany's words came to the forefront and became a welcomed melody floating through my mind: *"Just when you think you can't possibly survive, and the pain is too much to bear, that's when the baby comes."*

I had planned on having a natural birth, so I was somewhat

prepared. Somewhat. But this was insanity. The intensity and severity of the pain was something I never could have planned for, no matter how much I read or researched. With no time to change my plan to a medicated one, I lay there clenching everything...

My eyes, the rails, my stomach, Isaac's hand.

Every inch of me was trembling with the most intense pain I'd ever felt. I had Tiffany's words on a rhythmic cycle dancing through my mind. *When I think I can't possibly survive, that's when the baby comes. The miracle. The new life. Breathe. It's coming. I can do this. When the pain is too much to bear, that's when breakthrough happens.*

I clung to her words as if my very life and breath depended on it. And it very well may have.

Again and again in my mind like a looping record, I repeated, *When I think I can't possibly survive, that's when the miracle happens.* I sang these words to myself until a cry filled the air as fresh new lungs met earth for the very first time.

He came.

Our miracle.

I survived.

I burst into tears as my whole body collapsed onto the bed. I reached out my arms and melted into a puddle of praise as they placed him on my chest. Our little Logan Jude, our long-awaited miracle.

I couldn't stop crying as I checked him over. Every piece of his nine-pound, twenty-inch little frame. Ten fingers. Ten toes. Pouty little lips. Dark hair. His very name spoke truth and hope into our weary hearts as we stepped out into a new beginning from a dark and isolating chapter of our lives.

He was, and continues to be nearly four years later, an anthem of restoration, joy, and survival for our family. Our little Logan Jude, whose name means "from the hollow, we praise." From the dark, we continue to hope.

Through the pain, we keep going.

Logan Jude, our anthem.

Through the pain, WE KEEP GOING.

We made it, little one.

As I've walked in and out of different seasons and situations these last few years, I feel Tiffany's words on my very breath, infusing life into my dry and weary bones. When we think we are done, when we think it's over, when we can't possibly continue, when all hope is lost...it's then—no earlier, no later—that God leans down and births miracles through our mess.

And I'm so thankful to have had a front-row seat to this one.

10

First Dream

If you want to change the world, go home and love your family.

MOTHER TERESA

A few summers ago we spent the weekend at the coast with my dad. It was one of those times Norman Rockwell would have loved. Kids running with sticks, making forts, and roasting hot dogs on a driftwood fire. I took so many pictures I filled up my phone in just those few days.

But I wanted to remember everything. I didn't want to forget anything about that trip. The way the days felt, the smell of the fire, the crackle of the wood, the roar of the ocean, and the laughter of the children. I wanted to soak in every detail down to my deepest places.

We sat around the fire, talking about the kids and how Ava is just like Isaac and Isaiah is just like me. My dad started talking about how he and his sister are the same way. How he's exactly like his mom, and my aunt is exactly like my grandpa. I got a bit quieter as he continued to talk.

My dad started in on story after story of his parents' adventures. He's an amazing storyteller...he is gifted like that in a way I dream of being. So that day, like countless others, we sat and listened to his stories.

He talked all about his mother's love of travel, the time they spent on Orcas Island, and hitting the open road in their RV. As he spoke I felt my insides break apart a little that I didn't have more time with her.

My grandma and I clicked in ways I could never explain to anyone else, or even understand myself, for that matter.

She taught me to paint and to explore. I remember walking on the beach together for hours looking for shells and sand dollars and pretty agates as the seagulls flew overhead. It was our only time with just the two of us, and I truly treasure those moments I had with her. Something in me seemed to understand something in her, and maybe vice versa too. I guess I will never truly know.

Oh, how I wish she were still here. How I wish the dreamer I loved so much hadn't left so soon. To have missed out so much on a woman I barely knew but knew all too well became more devastating as my dad spoke and more of her heart and her fire came into focus.

I'm certain she would have some wisdom for me. Some little nuggets of truth that come from wrinkled skin and 40-plus years of marriage. I wonder what she'd tell me now. I wonder what we'd talk about if we could walk on that beach together one more time.

I started imagining what our conversations would be like if she were still here. Knowing her, I imagine she would say that you can never go wrong putting others' needs before yours. She would tell me to keep living and serving this beautiful family I have with all my heart. For having them is a dream fulfilled too. My first dream. She'd say that travels will come, and I may just end up with that Airstream someday. But today, today I have a family I love more than words and a husband I could kiss so much I just might suffocate him. And I need to cherish that too. I need to hold it so tight that I never lose sight of the beauty living under this roof.

She'd tell me that dreams are best when shared, but they can destroy you from the inside if that's all you're clinging to. So grab hold of what you have with all you've got. Hug them, cherish them, believe in, and encourage them.

TODAY is a MIRACLE bursting with POSSIBILITY.

Practice thankfulness every day, because they are your first dream. And the other dreams are up to God. Be a wife and mama first and a dreamer second. Because your family needs your feet on the ground as much as you need to soar. She'd say that time loving the people in our lives well is never, ever wasted. It's our first calling, to love well.

She'd say that God is faithful. Always faithful. And if something is meant to be, He will bring it about. But for now...for now I'm already living the dream. My first dream. So go cultivate that one, instead of longing for what could be.

The words I imagine her saying have been echoing in my heart and challenging me to embrace each season as its own. To be thankful for the time at home with little ones underfoot and the house always being messy. She'd challenge me to choose thankfulness again when they go off to school and I have a bit of breathing room.

I feel the intentional choice to embrace with gratitude what is, instead of longing for what could be, will be a battle I will fight all my life. I think we can all get trapped there if we let ourselves. Unable to love the life we've been given because we aren't yet experiencing the life we think we want. And if you're a dreamer, or creative, or a "what's next" thinker, this cycle is viciously more difficult.

But here is my challenge. Let's look around. Let's hold close what is sacred and true. Let's count those blessings, and kiss those cheeks, and say those prayers together. Let's choose to love this little life of ours with the fierce passion that brings glory to the Giver of all of these gifts in the first place.

Let's look around our home filled with train tracks, or tween magazines, or the stillness that comes when waiting for children or watching them go off to college, and soak it all in with gratitude and enjoyment.

Because whatever season it is we find ourselves in, God has us in it for a purpose, and He has a plan for our good. Whether the silence and waiting are shattering your heart, or the clutter and chaos are numbing your joy, today is a miracle bursting with possibility. A season that someday you will look back on, see the sweetness, and miss the moments.

This little life of ours.

These people we share it with.

These walls we laugh between.

It's all a miracle.

And it holds the power to change absolutely everything.

If we just choose to let it.

PART 2

Purpose

11

Vision Retreat

How we spend our days, is of course, how we spend our lives.

ANNIE DILLARD

How did I get here?

I stared at the spreadsheet in a daze, the numbers all blurring together in a mess of nonsense I was never created to understand.

All of my projects and businesses have begun because I simply had so much passion that I felt this burning, incessant desire to just jump in. I never really stopped to consider exactly what these new responsibilities would entail. But when the rubber hit the road, the workload quickly became overwhelming. I simply couldn't do all of the things, and certainly not do them well and efficiently. So, on top of the stress and panic I was feeling, the success of my endeavors began teetering on disaster as well. It wasn't long before I started down the path of ungratefulness, bitterness, and depression.

During that season I did anything and everything to keep these passions of mine oiled and running smoothly. Until one day I woke up, looked around, stared at my to-do list, and wondered, *How did I get here? Why am I doing spreadsheets all day when I can't make sense of them? It's like I'm trying to operate a business in a country where I can't read the language. Save me, please!*

I am an outside-the-lines gal. I don't do boxes, or order, or spreadsheets, or...chemistry, for that matter, so why was I doing any of this?

I sat dazed for several minutes in complete disbelief that this, in fact, was my life. And I started to shut down. *How did I get here?* I thought. *And, please, God, how do I get out?*

I must mention as a side note that I am well aware that there are going to be jobs we need to get done in our lives that don't light our fire. Like sweeping the floor, doing laundry, mailing out packages, or filing a never-ending stack of papers from our boss. I get that for sure. Sometimes things just need to get done, and it's up to us to pull on our boots, get to work, and do it well.

But this felt different. This felt like God wanted to get my attention for some reason. It suddenly seemed as if my world had gone off tilt, and I knew something had to change, but how?

The questions started swarming my soul in an unpleasant game of "What If?" And soon I became plagued with this massive guilt because my family had given up so much to support me as I chased these dreams. And yet, now I sat overwhelmed, broken, and unfulfilled, and wanting to quit all of them.

I needed to figure this out.

I needed a reset.

And I needed it yesterday.

In this moment, Proverbs 29:18 came to my mind, and *The Message* version hit hard on my heart. "If people can't see what God is doing, they stumble all over themselves; but when they attend to what he reveals, they are most blessed." The King James Version puts it, "Where there is no vision, the people perish."

In a single moment I realized that it had been a very, *very* long time since Isaac and I had sat down, reevaluated where things were in our businesses, our ministry, and our home, and actually sought God about them.

I had been saying yes to so many things, I didn't really know what made sense anymore, or why we were even making the decisions we were making. We didn't have a vision for anything, so no wonder I was stumbling all over myself!

Knowing we desperately needed to talk and pray together, I asked Isaac if I could set up a weekend away for us to go and seek God for our lives and businesses. Our anniversary is in January, so it fit perfectly with our annual weekend away and the feelings of new beginnings that accompany the New Year.

He was game, of course, so I booked a quiet cabin at a central Oregon resort, and a few weeks later we were on our way.

I'd like to say that those few days flowed together brilliantly like the swirling of my favorite coffee-and-vanilla-flavored coconut creamer. But it didn't exactly go down that way. Isaac is a doer, and not naturally a rester, while I tend to lean more toward the let's-stay-in-and-binge-watch-HGTV side of things. Neither of us were prepared for a sudden quiet, reverent, self-reflective weekend away from all of our responsibilities. And actually, it turned out to be way more awkward and difficult than we had initially thought. We hadn't given ourselves space like that in probably the entirety of our marriage. We always went away to do things or be with people. But this? This was hard. When we first got there, we sat silently for what seemed like forever, and I'm quite certain we were both thinking, *Uh? What do we do now?*

But somehow, even after the rocky beginning, this little weekend away felt truer in our souls than a hundred weekends before it. We spent the few days journaling by the fire, getting massages, and going on walks. We wrote down all of the victories and failures from the previous year and our hopes and dreams for the year ahead. We talked about what worked and what didn't, and the things we were scared to bring to the surface.

It was beautiful, and complicated, and hard. There were some tears, and many laughs, and just a whole lot of breathing room. It's amazing how much we were able to process and accomplish without the constant interruptions of beloved but disruptive little voices. We weren't needed anywhere, by anyone, and that was the most freeing part. We were able to dive into the heart of things that we hadn't had time for in way too long. We were able to talk about dreams we both felt the urge to pursue and to seek God together on what He had for our lives. But what struck me most was how this intentional time away helped us carve out new goals, and next steps, and direction for the days and years ahead.

And that, right there, is what held the magic for me.

It has been six years since that weekend away together, and we now make these getaways a tradition every January. It's become my favorite weekend of the entire year. I count down for it. I get excited. Expectant. Instead of waiting and pacing in our room for someone to speak first the way we did on our first vision retreat weekend, now we start talking about everything as soon as we kiss the kids good-bye and get into the car.

Time set apart is almost addictive when you know the power it holds. Life changing, to say the very least. You can't live in your mission or walk in your calling if you don't know what it is, where you're going, or the steps you need to take to get you there.

I don't want to overwhelm you, though. So I must let you in on a little secret. The tradition doesn't have to fit a rigid formula or be in a fancy resort. There are no molds to fit, just discoveries to be made. We've done this in snowed-in cabins an hour away, flown to Maui to feel the sunshine on our faces, and housesat for friends in San Diego while they were waiting to adopt in Africa. The setting is not nearly as important as the intention.

The simple act of taking time out of your schedule, intentionally and with purpose, to unify where you want your marriage and family to go is the win. That's the holy grail.

Taking the time to craft a vision for our family and our future is hands-down the best tool we've found in our entire marriage. Even if all you have is a friend's rental or a locals' rate for the hotel in your town, schedule a time to get away. Make this a priority. The place doesn't matter. It's the purpose that does. (But I'll be honest, beaches and cozy fireplaces aren't hurting anything either, am I right?)

Over the years we have calmed down a bit. Our time together is not awkward anymore. It's a breath of fresh air compared to that first weekend. We don't sit inside all day long journaling in front of a fireplace or forcing ourselves to read and listen to podcasts if we aren't in the mood. But that has more to do with us learning about *us*—and what brings us joy and helps us grow—than it does forfeiting the exercises.

Now we simply adventure together and seek God in the process. We do a little journaling, pray together, talk a lot, and make time to read the Word. But mostly we just spend time together, having fun and enjoying each other as we press into God for answers, clarity, and direction.

We sit by the pool, read, go on walks, eat good food, sleep in. Sometimes we meet up with good friends for coffee or go see a movie. But all the while, no matter what, we have these questions knocking around in our souls that we are determined to wrestle through.

And by the time we leave, we know where we are going and what we need to do next to get there. We know what we need to let go of and what we need to invest in.

The secret to all of it, though, is to remain pliable to His leading. We can't hold so tightly to our own dreams and desires that we aren't able to pivot when needed.

We must seek Him first. Lean into Him first. Listen to Him first. And from that, talk it out, let the dreams flow, process what your next steps should look like, and always, always write everything down!

Friend, the peace, joy, and passion that have been restored to us after just a few days away a year is unfathomable. God has used these weekends mightily—not only in our businesses, but in our marriage, our parenting, and the overall rhythms of our home. These retreats have clarified our direction and given accountability to our roles within our family and the businesses we run. Since we have a plan and core values to guide our decisions and divide our tasks, I'm no longer drained by responsibilities that I dread, or overwhelmed and weary because I said yes to things I didn't have margin for.

Our vision has given us permission to intentionally carve out the things that were weighing us down and hand them over to other people who excel in those areas. Like those blasted spreadsheets I was telling you about before.

And on the flip side, with the time I was saving by not doing those tasks, I was able to take on more roles and projects that really made me come alive, the things I like to believe I was created to do...like designing materials and events, mentoring leaders, and dreaming up new projects.

It's true that there is a time and a place in the beginning of a project or dream when you just have to buck up and do the work. Not every task is going to light your heart on fire. But after the wheels get turning and things are starting to move beyond you, there comes a point when you need to reevaluate your duties and your roles in the project. Being a good steward is about more than just money; it's also about how we spend our time and energy, and how we use our skills.

So why continue to spend ten hours on a project that would take someone else two? Take a deep breath, friend, and hand that task off to someone else who was designed to thrive in jobs like that. Pick up the things on the list that come so easy they don't even feel like work. Because that, friend, that's your sweet spot. That's the place you'll come fully alive, freely operating and thriving in your gifts, and making a huge impact on those around you and what you are working on.

There is something so sacred about taking time from our busy lives and intentionally committing it to grow in Him and connect with each other. We have dubbed the trip our annual "vision retreat"—and I admit that makes it sound a whole lot more sophisticated than it is. However, the naming was intentional, and an essential part of the process. It gave our time away a purpose. We could no longer use it as another fun weekend away, or a time to sleep in, or a chance to have an uninterrupted meal. Even though we did those things (and having an interruption-free conversation is pure gold), naming our time away gave it a purpose.

No one else has to answer for what you've been given to STEWARD

After experiencing so much freedom and joy from our vision weekends, there's not much that would bring me greater joy than for you to adopt this as a new tradition of your own. If you have ever found yourself wondering how on earth you got where you are or are confused about what to do next, I would encourage you to block out a few days and go on an adventure with God.

He has so much He wants to say to you, if only you quiet yourself to hear it.

And I, for one, cannot wait to hear what that is.

12

Pruning

*I have a vision of people everywhere having the courage to live
a life true to themselves instead of the life others expect of them.*

GREG MCKEOWN

Change is really hard.

Saying good-bye can be horrifically brutal.

And walking away from something you've poured your heart and
soul into for weeks, or months, or years can feel like an out-of-body
experience. Especially if you're the passionate, creative, productivity-
driven type. We builders tend to throw ourselves into our work in
incredibly intense ways.

For us, this passion project we'd taken on was hosting a women's
conference to help creative business women learn how to grow successful businesses and build a thriving home life. To add to the complex-
ities that already existed in running an event for hundreds of women,
we were also facing challenges of hosting said conference on the opposite side of the country from where we live and dealing with a retreat
center that didn't allow children.

What started as a simple gathering for entrepreneurial women to
connect, grow, and be equipped in their businesses and inspired in their
faith quickly took on a life of its own. We had team members scattered
across the country in different stages of life, and we had acquired the
most random collection of things that had very little purpose outside

of the conference world. And somewhere along the way I became the proud tenant of a huge storage unit in Rome, Georgia, to house all of this randomness. How on earth was this my life?

All of this was going on in what sometimes felt like an alternate universe while I plugged away at raising kiddos, supporting my hubby, and running my own businesses from our home in the Pacific Northwest.

Looking back, the insanity of it all makes me bust out in laughter. I mean, none of the other moms I knew were helping manage leaders in the Philippines and hosting events 3,000 miles away, but that was my normal. And I loved it.

As weird as it sounded when I explained it to strangers, it was my life, and it didn't seem one bit odd to me then. I was just following the next thing God had placed on my heart to do. And for years His hand and grace on it was so thick I could feel it. When we follow His lead, I've discovered that things that should be hard have a grace and ease to them. Not that they aren't difficult tasks, because they definitely are, but there's an almost tangible grace that covers you, and for years, I seemed to be walking right in the middle of it.

First Corinthians 2:9 promises that "no eye has seen, no ear has heard, and no mind has imagined what God has prepared for those who love him" (NLT), and after walking out this assignment, this verse suddenly had a bit of a comedic undertone.

Never in a million years would I have guessed that I'd be a girl running a worldwide ministry with a consistently sold-out conference across the country and maintaining a storage unit in the middle of Georgia, but somehow that's the position I found myself in.

I never doubted that the conference was something we were supposed to do. It always felt right. It felt like home. Until one day, it just didn't. It was almost as though the grace for it had suddenly lifted, and I started to feel like I had no idea what to do with myself anymore.

What used to be done easily, almost effortlessly, suddenly felt like a huge weight on my shoulders. I began stumbling all over myself and second-guessing everything. Looking back, I recognize this for what it was: having a lack of peace. But I didn't understand it then. I just knew things had massively shifted. Where I had previously been excited and passionate, exhaustion and pressure seemed to be taking up residence instead.

I started to feel unsettled on my insides and simultaneously guilty for dreading what God had obviously put His hand on for so many years. I was having trouble sleeping, and not in the "I'm so excited I just can't sleep" sort of way. This was more like "I'm so stressed I can barely breathe" kind of way. My health turned sideways, and panic attacks became a regular occurrence. I stopped smiling, and dancing. And singing in the shower turned into sob-fests as the warm water washed over my puffy eyes. My relationships started to suffer, my creativity was stifled, and for the first time in a really long time, I didn't even feel like me anymore.

I felt trapped. And scared. And like a complete and utter failure.

I knew hundreds of women who'd have loved to trade places with me and host this event, so that just made it all worse. All of a sudden, feeling like I couldn't handle it anymore seemed to cover me in a blanket of guilt and shame.

What would people think?

What would they say?

Who will I be if I don't do this?

The questions and pressure plagued my heart in a way I'd never experienced before, and the weight was a new kind of heavy. Everything I'd been working for, all that had been built, striven for, and wanted, was now so large that instead of freeing me, I was being crushed under the demands and responsibilities of it all.

And worse, managing it all felt like shackles keeping me from what God had been inviting me and my family into next.

As Jon Acuff says, "I was trapped in a cage I'd built myself." And now depression and anxiety had found their way in too.

There were so many things God had put on my heart, but my capacity was limited. I couldn't possibly start something new and continue the duties of running the conference with excellence at the same time. Unless, of course, I never slept or saw my family. And then what would be the point of running a ministry to help women build successful businesses and thriving families if I couldn't do it myself?

My heart ached and churned inside me at the magnitude of it all. The people it would affect. The businesses they ran. The families. The 200-plus small groups we had around the world that included nearly 25,000 people.

What would they all think?

Or would they even care?

The thought of failing them, or, on the flip side, being invisible and not even noticed, was nearly crippling me. I found myself withdrawing in every sense of the word as I processed it all. I couldn't answer phone calls. I couldn't post on social media. Some days I couldn't even get out of bed. Although I guess that's not true, because when you have three kids depending on you for getting through the day, you get out of bed whether you feel like it or not.

But I was empty. Broken from the inside out. And the light and bubbly dancing-in-the-kitchen self that used to overflow out of me had been snuffed and silenced.

It felt like a lose-lose situation. Even though I know God has our best in mind, it certainly didn't feel like it during those days.

I feared all the things, all at once. But I feared for my own family the most. How could I tell them it wasn't worth it anymore? How could I look them in the eye and say, "You know all those nights Mommy worked, all the money we poured into this ministry, all of those weeks away from you that I'd spent leading events? Well, it's all a loss. Mommy doesn't want to do it anymore."

Picturing this conversation brought tears to my eyes and a gut-wrenching burden to my soul. I couldn't walk away from this. I just couldn't do that to them. They'd given up so much for me. And for Pursuit. How selfish could I possibly be?

A few months after I first felt the tug to shut down the conference, I was pruning one of the apple trees in our orchard, as we do every winter. I sat among the almost naked limbs as the crisp, cold wind whipped across my face, and I hacked away at the branches.

One by one, I watched these budding little twigs fall to the ground. There were hundreds of them. Each full of life with fresh cotton candy–pink buds ready to burst forth from their green buds in the coming weeks. Each cut I made left a bright green and white scar on the tree, proving there was no death in those branches.

The limbs I was cutting were fully alive, strong, thriving, and dripping with potential fruit.

In an instant I heard the Lord speak to my heart: "See, I'm not always asking you to just cut away things that are unhealthy and dying. It's not just the things that drain your heart and leave you emotionally and financially bankrupt that need to be reevaluated. Sometimes I'm asking you to cut off pieces that are actually alive and thriving. Because sometimes those things are sucking the energy from the most important places, the better investments."

Immediately a warm peace flooded my body, and in that moment I knew I had been hearing Him clearly all along.

The conference wasn't a bad thing. It was actually a great thing. A gloriously fruitful thing. But it had fulfilled what the Lord had wanted it to, and I needed to be as faithful to obey when He asked me to walk away as I was when He asked me to start. It was now time to close the door on that season and put that energy into other dreams God had been whispering to my heart.

As another limb bursting with buds fell to the ground, I began to cry. Relief and peace filled the places in my heart where burdened responsibility and paranoia resided moments before. Goodness, nature is such a beautiful glimpse into the character of God.

The seasons, the cycles, the undeniable rhythms.

Isn't it amazing how the very best thing you can do for fruit trees is cutting off all of the suckers during winter?

And how interesting is it that they are even called suckers in the first place? Since they are sucking life from the other parts of the tree that need it to produce fruit?

Later that day Isaac initiated a conversation as we sat down for lunch. "Babe? What would you do if I said you didn't have to do the conference anymore?"

His blunt words shocked me, and it took a minute to process the magnitude of his question just hours after my pruning encounter. I sat there silenced and in complete disbelief that he was bringing up the subject. Under my breath I remember speaking these words: "I would cry tears of happiness. And instantly feel like a million pounds were just lifted off of my shoulders."

I stared down at my plate, using my fork to move around my food.

Without hesitation he replied confidently, "Well, then that's what we are going to do."

You're saying I can walk away? I thought.

Instantly I felt like I could breathe a full breath for the first time in months, if not years. Upon hearing those words, the stress and anxiety that had been suffocating me lifted. I don't think I will ever forget that moment as long as I live.

My word, I love that man.

Looking back, the pressure, stress, depression, and lack of peace should've been warning signs to get the heck out. And if you're currently feeling any of those about your situation, maybe they should be for you too.

But I've never been the first one to hit the brakes on anything. When I start something, I finish it. Usually long past the time it's healthy to. My over-responsible personality and my addiction to productivity don't let me entertain the thoughts of walking away from something. Especially something that is extremely successful.

But what I'm learning is that sometimes when your heart feels as though it's drying up, it's not that you've failed; it's that God is telling you to move into a new season.

GRACE.

IT was all just

GRACE.

Within 36 hours of my conversation with Isaac about shutting down the conference, my phone rang. It was a woman from the storage unit in Georgia. "Ma'am, we've had a flood, and your unit is a complete loss. We have been given 24 hours to evacuate the premises and have everything out of all units. There was nothing we could do. The entire facility was buried in four feet of water, and now we need you to get your stuff out. What do you want to do?"

"Uh...what?" I said. "I live on the West Coast. I can't possibly get all of my stuff out within 24 hours!" The lady seemed a bit shocked that I was so far away, despite the fact that she was looking at my rental agreement and could see my address.

I hung up the phone in complete disbelief. *You've got to be kidding me*, I thought. I didn't know whether to laugh or cry, and in the end, I did a little bit of both. I laughed at the insane improbability of our storage facility (which had been advertised as 100 percent waterproof) flooding, and even funnier...flooding from a stream behind the building named "Little Dry Creek." Nearly six years' worth of equipment, décor, table settings, backgrounds, projection screens, and who knows what else that had accumulated in that ten-by-ten space—somewhere between ten and fifteen thousand dollars of stuff. Lost in an instant.

And to top it off, the insurance company, in true insurance company fashion, found a loophole to escape covering any of it. They didn't pay a single dime.

Through it all, though, we felt the hand of God was at work and that this was a divine confirmation we were walking in the right direction. And it was finally time to prune this sucker too.

I wish I could say that the events that followed were as confirming and divine as the events that unfolded to set us into motion, but that's just not the case. It turns out that when you do anything that involves other humans, those other humans almost always have opinions. And it's not always awesome.

While the majority of the women in Pursuit were overwhelmingly sweet and supportive, this massive change in the direction of the ministry didn't go without opposition. When I began to share my heart and what God was leading us to do, it felt as if I'd invited everyone else to weigh in with their opinions. Which I had not.

I began to realize that when God speaks a direction into our lives, the enemy will quickly come and bombard us with many other voices in an effort to cause confusion and derail us from our destinies. Not all voices are bad, but it does take discernment and prayer to weed through the words. If you're ever in a similar situation, remember to filter the words of others through God's character, His Word, and His truths. Take into account where these voices are coming from. Remember that 5,000...12...3...1 thing we talked about? That is very applicable here. Are they random strangers, acquaintances, or a trusted confidant whose relationship with God you can trust? After you've filtered the voices and the verbiage, you can keep the gold and throw out the garbage.

The biggest tool for all of it is to hold fast to what is true. Cling to the One who led you into this decision and what He is inviting you into. Because no one else has to answer for what you've been given to steward. There will always be naysayers, those who say you can't hear God or that you heard Him wrong. But sometimes those voices are the exact confirmation you're on the right path. Because why would the enemy want to discourage you from the wrong path?

Opposition is often confirmation that you're going in the right direction.

So, friend, I guess what I'm saying in all of this is to keep going. People who say you can't hear God are wrong. His sheep know His voice. You know His voice. So hang in there. Lean in. Get closer. Feel His breath on your face as He whispers the way of what's to come. Quiet your heart. Open your hands. Let go of what He's asking you to. Walk away.

A door closed isn't a loss; it's a launching pad to what's next.

So hold fast to Him.

Lean in close as He leads.

He won't ever steer you wrong.

And He's probably getting ready to open the floodgates on that part of your tree that most needs tending.

13

Bridge Builders

Be kind, for everyone is fighting a hard battle.

IAN MACLAREN

"Maybe we are supposed to go on a road trip over spring break," I said in passing, almost hoping Isaac wouldn't hear me.

He heard me.

"What?" he said. "We can't afford that. Why would we do that?"

"I need to see them," I said. "I need to make things right again."

I wish I could say that I was always this eager for reconciliation. That the right thing to do always comes easy for me, and every thought I have toward people who have wronged me is holy. But that's simply not the case.

This particular day, though, I was overwhelmed with a deep need to take action in a relationship that had gone silent, and I knew that being face-to-face was the only way to rebuild the bridge.

This world isn't always as kind as we wish it was, and sometimes the people closest to us aren't either. The tensions in a friendship can be amplified all the more when you are working in the same industry, targeting the same clients, or creating similar products. Labels usually meant for competitors are suddenly sitting across the table from you offering you a cup of coffee and asking you about your kids.

Business and friendship together are a strange phenomenon. One that takes careful treading to navigate well. But, as is usually the case, the things that take the most work and have the potential to break our hearts the most are often worth the most amount of work and time.

This isn't a shiny, happy part of our story that I love sharing with people. It's extremely embarrassing and even a bit shameful. But I feel it would be a disservice to hide it and thus hold back even a glimpse of hope for others facing similar situations.

So here it goes.

Isaac and I have been through a lot of relational hurt during our married years. I'm not exactly sure what that says about us. Maybe we wear our hearts too loosely on our sleeves, or trust too soon, or are just extremely naïve. Maybe we are dumb, or too sensitive, or we have giant flashing signs on our foreheads that blink, "Walk all over us...we can take it!"

However you unpack it, we've had more than our fair share of friends who've decided that integrity wasn't their game after all. When push came to shove, they just haven't chosen to do the right thing. We've been stolen from, lied to, betrayed, walked away from, mocked, and yes, even excommunicated. If that's even a real thing anymore. Which it certainly feels like it is.

And for two people who will lay it all down on the altar of integrity, this not choosing to do things with integrity is a particularly vicious poison.

Sadly, through it all, we have become masters of self-protection. Over the years we constructed a fairly secure wall around our hearts— and our home, for that matter. For years it was all we could do to keep our hearts pumping, let alone open them up to another potentially hazardous soul. Plus, the strength and control that we harvested from our isolated lifestyle became a deceptive confirmation that our choice to wall off humanity was a wise one.

We were safe inside our walls. And that brought a welcomed, albeit harmful, sense of peace. Well, maybe not peace, but security.

We were safe.

We were extremely lonely, but we were safe.

And in those years we were willing to trade nearly anything to feel safe.

As sad as this was, this new routine quickly developed into a family rhythm that was too comforting to let go. When you wall off your heart and burn bridges instead of build them, you are guaranteed a few things. Security and safety were the big ones for us, but they came at the extremely high and unexpected price of isolation, depression, and severe loneliness.

A few years ago one friendship in particular took a hefty blow. At least to our hearts. I honestly don't even know if this friend of ours felt they did anything wrong. And I guess it doesn't even matter if they did.

Because I felt it.

Isaac and I both did.

We felt overwhelmingly wronged. Despite our giant barrier walls, betrayal had infiltrated our world again from someone we had actually welcomed and trusted to come inside our walls of protection.

It's hard to know what you'll do in any particular situation until you're in it. You believe you'll react responsibly and carry through with every ounce of forgiveness you claim on Sunday mornings. But when the layers peel off and the ick is exposed, repairing relationships doesn't always seem worth it.

And even though it felt like a hurricane was hovering over my insides, on the surface I appeared as calm and peaceful as a lake in the early morning. As countless people begged me to drag their names through the mud or cut them off completely, something in my heart defended them. Some piece of me knew there was a deeper story playing out. I just didn't know what it was yet.

After the story of what happened was revealed, it was nearly a year before we spoke again. Their family had their lives, and we had ours. We were both navigating the throes of whatever had found its way into our homes, and we were both just doing the best we could to steward it all. In fact, that phrase became something I clung to fiercely in this season—that we were all doing the best we could.

In our little perfect worlds, with our Nicholas Sparks romances and our storybook endings, it's easy to be thrown off-kilter when life doesn't go our way. Or worse, when relationships don't. We can so easily be tempted to run, hide, cut off, or at our very worst, talk horribly about people to others.

But none of that is what we truly want, is it? We don't want to be the girl dragging someone else's name through the mud, or be unable to take a joke or forgive or move on. We wouldn't want a friend like that, yet so many of us insist on *being* a friend like that.

Hurts, offenses, and bad blood don't just happen. We aren't born feeling those things. They have to be let in. Oftentimes we blame these poisonous feelings on others, but the truth is, it's not their fault. We hold the keys to the doors of our hearts. And we hold the power to keep things out, and let things in.

Bitterness came knocking fiercely the night we discovered what had happened. And every night after, for that matter. But something in me couldn't let it in. Someone might call it naïveté, but I think compassion feels like a better fit. I don't mean to sound super spiritual, but all I could picture was Jesus at the Passover supper.

As we've discussed already, I'm a feeler. And a visionary. So when I picture something, I picture all the things. And I feel them as if I were walking through it all firsthand. I'm the one crying at all of the commercials and plugging my ears to the evening news. I just imagine things so vividly that I must protect my heart from the stories I let in.

The same thing happens when I read the Bible, or any other story, for that matter. So when I think about Jesus and the Last Supper, I picture the room He and His disciples were in and the people around the table. I picture the bread they broke, and the clothes they wore, and imagine how it all smelled. How it all felt.

And then I picture Him. Our Savior. I picture Jesus seated with the 12 people who were His dearest, closest friends on this earth. I picture the conversations and the silence that fell when He mentioned someone at the table would betray Him.

GOD has PUT these things on your heart FOR A PURPOSE and most likely a purpose far greater THAN YOU.

I picture the panicked looks on their faces, and I picture the grace on His.

And as all of this played out in my mind's eye, I instantly knew why this offense was so hard for me to pick up. Even when everyone around me was encouraging me to do just that.

It was grace.

It was all just grace.

If Jesus could invite someone to His last meal on earth knowing that person would betray Him, then certainly I have no room, or right, to hold on to the offense of being betrayed by a friend. Even though I had held hurt and carried contempt for this situation, I knew it wasn't right to do so. I knew it was time to lay it down. To let it go.

And to build a bridge instead.

A few weeks later we loaded up the whole family, all five of us, in our black SUV and hit the freeway—games loaded, snacks packed, hearts open and full of peace, knowing what we had to do. Nearly 900 miles and 20 hours later, between full bladders and hungry bellies, we arrived.

As we greeted each other at breakfast the next morning, I didn't exactly know what to expect. Would we talk about it? Would they apologize? Would we move on like it never happened? Even though the questions were looming in my mind, I knew I wasn't there for an apology or a ceremony of forgiveness. It just didn't matter anymore. I loved them like family, and I didn't need to hear an apology. I had already decided that no matter what happened in the past, I still wanted us to have a future. Together.

Tragically, I think it is common in our culture to wait for someone else to do the right thing before we are willing to. We want them to make it right before we choose to move on. We want an apology before we can forgive.

But the gospel just doesn't operate that way.

And we, as kingdom carriers, shouldn't either.

As much as I wish it didn't work this way, forgiveness is an action, not a feeling. As many times as I've forgiven people over the course of my life, I can't remember a single time when I *felt* like forgiving them.

It's always been, at least the best my memory is allowing me to recall at the moment, a very intentional choice. And only after the choice do the feelings follow. And sometimes the feelings take an incredibly long time to line up to your choice. At least that's been true for me.

As we got together that morning, we all hugged and sat at tables as the kids played nearby. We laughed and told stories and had awkward pauses where I'm sure we both wanted to bring up the situation but didn't. All the while, with every word and forgiving glance, we were laying boards, mending ropes that were almost worn through, and choosing to build up rather than tear down.

Peace flooded over me like an ocean wave that day, and without saying so, we all knew a page had turned. It's crazy the giddiness that fills your heart when you partner with grace and say no to offense. So often we want God to use us mightily for the kingdom, but then we don't want to roll up our sleeves and get dirty in the messes that come with it. But the reality is, love is messy. It's not tidy or convenient, and it certainly doesn't always need tending at the exact time we have the capacity to tend it. We have to make time for what we know is right.

When Jesus built the bridge between us and God through His death on the cross, it became the messiest love ever recorded. And the world is still being washed in the wake of it.

It was tearstained, blood-covered, flesh-torn-open, and most definitely not convenient. It was a choice to forgive, a choice to surrender, a choice to give grace, a choice to trade His will for the Father's, and a choice to lay down His life for ours.

All in the name of the greatest love we will ever know.

He paid the ultimate price to build a bridge for us. To let bitterness, and sin, and ugliness, and selfishness drown in the wake of love.

And now it's our duty and our honor as believers to do the same.

To live a life where the wake of His love, through our actions, covers all.

And ultimately to build bridges, through our love, from a lost world to Him.

14

Mouths of Babes

*Having a parent that listens creates a child who believes
he or she has a voice that matters in this world.*

RACHEL MACY STAFFORD

Being a mama is insanely hard work. Raising tiny people to become responsible adults is Blow. Your. Mind. Challenging. Whether you're in the wiping stage, constantly tending bottoms and noses and faces and mirrors and counters, or you're learning how to handle an empty nest and random phone calls with your grown little loves who are now on their own, nothing I have found is more challenging, or rewarding, as being a mama.

With a teenager, a tween, and a preschooler, I find peanut butter stains and piles of laundry feeling more like home than clean floors and pretty candles. Juggle that with having to actually get dressed in real clothes to watch a choir performance or a football game, and it's enough to make me wave my flag of surrender altogether.

It's tough, and exhausting. Most days I don't even feel like myself because I'm just so tired. But the ticking of the clock and the gravity of how short our time together really is has caused me to shift almost everything in the last few years.

I adore what I do, and the work I get to throw myself into feels like a gift to my soul and breath to my lungs. But I have to be careful not to let it completely overtake my heart and leave the people I love most without a mama who's actually paying attention.

It's a fight to keep my head in the mom game most days. It doesn't give out awards and accolades the same way a business success does. But the fruit of a well-tended family goes so far beyond the fruit of a well-tended business.

This season we are in has me pressing my face up against the windows of my own home and reevaluating everything. I'm learning that I need to be my children's mama first and everything else second. I need to spend an hour a day on the computer for work instead of ten. I need to put down my phone and seize the moments. Push the swing. Let them help with dinner. Show them how to paint, use a power drill, and plant a garden.

It's time to put down my checklist and take back their childhood.

As the lines on the growth chart get higher and higher, and their eyes are getting closer and closer to looking straight into mine without a stepping stool, I'm reminded that the seeds we plant in their tiny little hearts will become huge plants one day. Plants that bear fruit and take on lives of their own.

It's caused me to wonder if they will bear fruit of love, joy, peace, patience, kindness, goodness, gentleness, faithfulness, and self-control. Or will the seeds we are planting and watering inside them grow into fear, sorrow, confusion, frustration, isolation, meanness, infidelity, and indulgence?

I've been convicted of this a lot lately, and I feel blessed that I have been. Because if I hadn't, I may have missed an opportunity a while back that went on to affect thousands of families around the world. But it started with simply showing Isaiah that his voice mattered and that his ideas, his God nudges, were worth pursuing.

A few years back, our son Isaiah, who was seven at the time, came and sat with me at the kitchen table as I was having my quiet time and planning my day. I was filling in the prompts in the *Intentional Days Journal* I'd created a few months before, and Isaiah found it the perfect time to cozy up next to me and fill his quality-time, physical-touch love language.

My calling is not a SPECIFIC accomplishment; it's what I was MADE TO DO.

I continued writing, reading, and answering all the questions he had about what I was up to while rubbing his back with my other hand. He was very invested and curious, and oddly, it was one of those mysterious times where I knew in my spirit it was time to pay attention.

"Mom, can I have a journal like that?" he asked. "I want to have a place to write all of those things just like you do."

"Of course!" I responded, quickly affirming him. I offered him one of the extra journals I had in the garage. But since they were adorned with beautiful hand lettering and pink peonies throughout, he kindly refused and glanced back at me with the cutest, slightly grossed-out grin.

Knowing the one I had at home wasn't an option, we opened the computer and began searching for kids' quiet time journals, and to our surprise, we didn't find any. There were lots of devotionals for kids, and tons of books and Bibles, but nothing as interactive as what we were looking for. "It doesn't look like there are any, buddy," I said. "But I will keep looking, and if I find something, I'll see if it's something you'd like."

Without even hesitating, Isaiah said, "What if we make one, Mama? Like the one you made, but for kids? Could we do that?"

I was a little startled at his initiative and passion, but I had a choice in that moment to lean in or let it pass by. I easily could have said, "You know what, buddy? That's a great idea, but that's a really big project. I don't think it's something we can do."

But something inside me didn't let that happen. My Holy Spirit meter was telling me this was one of those moments that could change so much for his little heart. What I didn't realize at the time was how much it would do for mine.

It had been a rough year for him at school, and his sensitive soul was still recovering from the sting of it all. This project felt like the perfect way for us to do something fun together, and for him to feel like his ideas were valuable and worth investing in.

I pulled out a bunch of copy paper and laid it out on the table. I got a pen and some colored pencils and asked him to mock up some pages with the questions he wanted to ask. Ava, who was nine then, joined in the party too. And soon our whole family was around the table dreaming up ideas and collaborating on the new project.

The next thing I knew I had jumped onto Photoshop and turned their sketches into digitalized pages. While I was doing that, I had them both draw their own covers for their personalized journals. Then we scanned them, and within a few hours I had uploaded the pages to a website to get their very own custom journals printed.

When the journals arrived, the kids loved them so much that sitting down for daily quiet times together became a quick habit and a welcomed ritual. And the conversations that were sparked during our times together became my absolute favorite part of our day.

By this time, my entrepreneurial brain was spinning, and I couldn't help but think that if we were enjoying them so much, there must be other families who'd enjoy them too. I texted my dear friend Jordanne, who'd previously told me that she had dreamed of illustrating children's books, and asked if she could help me bring this project to life. I had a vision of creating characters that kids could get attached to and feel comfortable with. I thought it fitting that these cute little critters would lead them in their adventure of faith.

After a few hundred texts and several rough sketches, we'd honed in on the concept, and Archer the fox and his band of friends were born. With a few more texts and some idea mapping, the first Adventures with Archer journals were officially underway.

Since that day, we've gone on to release and sell out of five versions of the journals. One for every season and a special Advent version. We've shipped thousands of copies to families all over the world, and it never gets old seeing photos of children I've never met experiencing their own quiet times because of this tool! And honestly, it's all because of Isaiah's sweet little heart, and my pausing long enough to actually notice.

The magic of this story is that things like this don't just happen.

They are intentionally tended. Instead of simply nodding my head and not really paying attention, I had to be present enough to truly listen to Isaiah. And then, when he spoke, I had to stop what I was doing and engage with his idea. When the idea started to take root, I had to do design work on the computer and call in reinforcements for the illustrations. I had to invest countless hours of time and research, and thousands of dollars in production and design costs.

There were many, many steps that took us from a fun conversation one morning to launching a complete children's book series with customers all over the world. But it all started with making the intentional choice to lean in and listen. To wake up and pay attention to what was unfolding right before my eyes.

And I'm so thankful I didn't miss it.

Our children are gifted, friend. So very gifted. They ache to be seen just as we all do. That longing is not something that appears out of nowhere as we grow; it's always there. Praying and hoping for a chance to do something great or think of something world changing. And our kids have the ability to change the world tucked in their tiny hearts.

It's time for them to see us seeing them. To give them credit, and opportunity, and applause. To give them a chance to succeed instead of assuming they'll fail. Sometimes it's pushing aside our own mindset: "Their ideas can't be as good as ours, so why even try?" Or "We have so much going on we can't possibly take the time to sow into such an involved project."

I'd love to say that I'm always this attentive and that every idea that bursts out of my children's mouths gets as much attention as that one did. But that's not true. The truth is, not every idea is even good enough to tend, but it *is* good enough to be heard attentively. It's not as easy as jumping into every whim they have. And I certainly wouldn't have taken all of this so far if the Holy Spirit hadn't prompted me to and my husband hadn't supported me. So please, oh please, don't throw common sense and wisdom out the window in pursuit of being a supportive mom.

But I do want to challenge you to truly pay attention. To look up from what you're doing and not only listen to them, but to truly hear them. And act on what you're hearing. Keep looking them in the eye. Keep praying over the words, and dreams, and ideas that come blubbering out of their little hearts. And ask the Father what to do with it all.

It might just surprise you.

And the whole world too.

15

Never-ending

*While we wait for our callings to present themselves,
they are waiting on us to wake up.*

JEFF GOINS

My life seems to ebb and flow between the waves of ideation, productivity, and fulfillment of the dreams God places on my heart. It's what keeps me up at night and makes me come alive. If I feel the urge to lay something down, it's just a matter of time—usually not even a few hours—before I've dreamed up something else to fill the blank hours of my days.

It's almost as if I'm addicted to the process of it all. Which I probably am.

And this cycle of crazy nearly became the end of me about a year ago after laying down the conference. One day I woke up in a panic, not sure of who I was or what I was to do now that I didn't have huge to-do lists and thousands of e-mails to respond to.

Who am I if I'm not running this event? I wondered. I had been doing it so long that it almost became my identity. And actually, I completely feared that it had.

Am I even valuable? Will people even care? Is everything I've worked for gone in an instant? Does it even matter what I do from here? Will I just be forgotten? The more I allowed these thoughts to swirl around in my head, the faster they seemed to come.

Have you ever felt that way? Like you wouldn't matter if you weren't doing your job, or being productive, or making great strides toward your dreams?

For months after I made the decision to close the conference, I found my thoughts arguing back and forth with each other. On one hand I felt solid, secure, and at peace with the decision we'd made.

On the other, I was fighting off all of the thoughts telling me how much I'd failed, that I had no purpose, and that nothing I did ever mattered. And by the way, even if it had mattered, I was convinced it certainly wouldn't anymore. The battle in my mind was fierce and constant, and would have taken me out completely if I'd let it.

But I knew that the Lord promises to draw near to us if we draw near to Him. I begged God to speak because my own thoughts were simply too much to navigate on my own. It wasn't long before I began to ponder, *What actually is a calling anyway? Is it my job? Is it this conference? Or is it possibly something completely different?*

I started diving into the Word and researching everything I could on calling, and purpose, and assignments, and even though it's become a popular topic in the Christian culture, it's not exactly an easy thing to figure out. Romans 1:6 (ESV) says, "including you who are called to belong to Jesus Christ." And Romans 8:28 says, "We know that in all things God works for the good of those who love him, who have been called according to his purpose."

So we know that we are called to belong to Christ and that we are called according to His purpose. There were also stories of God calling others into specific things, but the Bible doesn't write out in black and white that Jenny is called to be an accountant, and Logan a fireman, and Billy a missionary. So it made me wonder if calling is something entirely different from what I've believed most of my life.

I started wondering if maybe my calling wasn't a specific thing I had accomplished or would accomplish but more about what I was created to spend my life doing. More specifically, I began to wonder if a *calling* goes on forever, while a *commission* is something that starts and ends.

The more I explored this theory, the more I realized that there seems to be a wide belief in our society that our calling is found in what we do. That being a teacher, or a writer, or even a mom is our greatest calling. But if that's the case, what happens to our calling when those jobs end? Or when our kids grow up and leave the house? Somewhere along the line, we as a culture decided that we had to put a destination around our calling. As if it were a specific job that could be explained in an elevator-pitch introduction.

The more God invited me into this conversation with Him, the more I started to think that our cultural beliefs about calling are likely a vast misconception. And I'm starting to feel that what we do is just a snippet of our calling and a teensy portion of our purpose. To me it's a fleeting glimmer of our days here on earth, but there is so much more to factor into our stories.

If we are one of the lucky ones, what we do will actually be an extension of what we love. But that's not always the case. And if you aren't one of those souls who's magically turned their passion into their profession, there is still hope. Because I'm starting to think that our calling has nothing to do with the words that make up our job descriptions, and everything to do with who we actually are and how we go about any job or duty.

In my own life this has been a mind-blowing epiphany. I found myself asking questions like, "Who am I really? What am I here for? What are the things I do no matter what form they take on? How does what I am here for look when my jobs change?"

When I began to separate *ministry leader* and *conference director* from the lines behind my name, I felt simultaneously empty and deeply fulfilled. Staring back at me, in black and white, were two words. My name. *Karen Stott*. Who was I then? With no words and accolades following my name?

When I stripped my name of titles and opened up blank space behind my name, God started writing a new story in me. He began to drop words into my heart that felt as familiar as my small hometown in Oregon's wine country.

Words like *builder, encourager, innovator, beautifier*. I began to write them out, and it wasn't long before I saw patterns unfold that had nothing to do with job titles or task lists and everything to do with who I was, and *why* I believe I was created and put here during this age and time in the first place.

These are the words that I had scribbled out on the page:

I like to start things.

I see greatness in others, and I help them see it in themselves.

I have an innate gift to help others walk in the fullness of their calling and make something from nothing.

I have a deep love, and knack, for making bland things beautiful and people feel seen.

I am an experience curator and a calling cultivator.

As these words poured out, a deep sense of YES fell over me. YES! This! This is what I am here for! This is what I was made to do, made to be.

And the best part is that I can do all of those things in any position, or job, or season.

I do them with my kids, and with my friends, and in any position I've been placed.

And I think that's what makes our calling so wonderful.

Most likely, we are already doing it.

We just might not even know that we are.

I think we need to take a moment to pause and take the pressure off of ourselves. Oftentimes I feel like I've missed it. Like I've messed up so big that I've not only missed it for me, but I've missed it for my children too. I get down on myself for not having this grand life's work, like a professor, or an inventor, or a doctor. Those people always felt superior in my mind because they knew what they were passionate about, what they were good at, and they dedicated their life to it.

To me, they had found their purpose.

IF GOD IS
calling you
to something
that doesn't
MAKE SENSE,
you're in
good
COMPANY.

That was it. End of story.

And for me, the crazy gal who never could quite land the plane, this whole finding my calling and fulfilling my purpose thing felt completely out of reach. And I was just out of luck.

But as I leaned into God, He began to reveal to me another side of the story.

And I must admit, being the daughter of a retired teacher and the wife of a man starting to look at what his life will be after firefighting helped this process immensely.

Isaac has the most incredible service heart I've ever seen. I've never met such an attentive, self-motivated need-meeter in my life. He just notices things. He has this knack of being able to survey a situation, see the needs, and know how to fix the problem or meet the need.

My mom, who taught for over 40 years in our community's schools, has an incredible gift of helping others understand things. She has a gift of communication, and knowledge, and revealing the gifts and abilities in people that they might not know are there.

Both for my mom, and for Isaac, their jobs are simply an extension of who they are anyway. And walking out of those titles won't hinder their callings in the slightest. It simply gives them new opportunities to use those gifts in a different setting.

I have been able to encourage, and beautify, and cultivate callings, and see greatness in others as a child growing up, as a wife, a mama, a ministry leader, a photographer, an author, and a shop owner.

Because *that* is who I am. It's who God has created me to be.

And I will be able to continue doing those things no matter what specific commissions, or jobs, or paths, or opportunities God leads me in and out of.

Isn't that so freeing? So beautiful?

What are those things for you?

I've heard it said that our calling is where our strengths and our passions collide, and I couldn't agree more. When I read those words on the paper I can almost feel the fire rekindling and the joy resurfacing.

Seeing what I have always had, and will continue to have regardless of a specific position, overwhelms my heart with all the good feelings.

And I hope it does for you too.

Every word of what I wrote in the list a few pages back is a passion of mine or a strength I have discovered along the way. And I've found so much beauty and rightness in both.

Seeing who I really am unfold in black and white helped me realize that running a conference and leading a ministry wasn't really my calling after all. Those were simply commissions in a series of probably a dozen or more commissions that I will walk through over the course of my life.

When my commission as a conference director ends, my calling continues. It just takes on different forms. When my children grow up and move out of our home, my calling doesn't graduate with them. It just morphs into something else.

A burden lifted off my shoulders as the words God had whispered to my heart took up residence in my soul. Knowing that I get to use my gifts and walk in my calling in our home, and with our kids, and with Isaac, and in whatever work God leads me into was a welcomed breath of fresh air. But knowing that laying down the conference wasn't the end to my story was also a welcomed relief.

I think we all have this ache inside of us that longs for something bigger, something grand. We want to be a part of the larger picture, and have our lives stand for something that matters, and build things that last.

And the beautiful part about all of that is that each commission God leads us into is simply a role in that larger story. It's a stepping stone. A preparation.

It's divinely placed. Specifically timed with an eternal purpose that weaves all of these commissions together and allows us to live our greatest, wholly present, fullest, joy-brimming lives that create a tapestry to reflect His greatness.

I say this, friend, because I know the joy of starting a new adventure and the ache of watching it come to a close. I've opened businesses and closed them. I've started new friendships and watched them fizzle. I've had thousands in savings and I've received stacks of overdraft letters from the bank. I've built houses, sold them, and even lost them. I've had great successes and great failures.

I have loved, and I have lost.

Through it all, the beauty I've held on to is knowing that the Lord gives and takes away, but who I am, and who HE is, and what I've been called to do while I'm here...those things remain.

No matter what, God is faithful.

No matter what, He will work good in my story.

No matter what, I will praise Him in it.

No matter what, He will always be there.

No matter what, I will encourage others to follow Him.

No matter what, He is good and kind.

No matter what, I will build and make beautiful.

And that is what calling is. Remaining faithful to who He's created us uniquely to be and following Him into commissions, and out of them as well.

Step by step, season by season, commission by commission, we are called to use how He wove us to step into the good works He's already prepared in advance for us to do.

No matter what.

Shekels

Face the fear of today, instead of regret forever.

JON ACUFF

Fear is one of those words that I kind of despise.

It's everywhere these days in a way that almost discredits its actual ugliness. It feels like it's sneaking its way into our everyday language to the point that we aren't appalled when it's brought up anymore. "Conquer your fears," we're told. "Look your fears in the face." "Feel the fear, and do it anyway."

It's unending, borderline annoying, and most likely on a hand-lettered shirt in your closet. I get it. I do. But it's almost like fear is one of those prickly underwater corals that has been sanded down so much that it feels like a Ping-Pong ball against your skin.

Where did the ugly parts of fear go?

What happened to the horrifying reality of what our lives would look like in 50 years if we let fear win? I feel that before we can actually do something about this new and improved "fear," we actually need to get a little real with it. We need to take off the pretty clothes of the "acceptable" fear we allow ourselves to have and break it down a bit.

Here's the thing. We aren't born with fear. It's not something we naturally take in and own. It's placed upon us repeatedly as we learn what it's like to be human in this world.

I can still remember what my life was like before fear entered the picture.

I was raised on about 50 acres in the Middle of Nowhere, Oregon. My daddy was a logger, and up the hill from our house, around a winding gravel road, sat his log mill. I can still hear the sound of him cutting timber and smell the greasy-oily aroma of chain saws mixed with the wet, earthy scent of freshly cut wood.

I remember how warm my grandpa's green metal coffee thermos felt in my cold, wet hands. The way he would drive me around in the front seat of his truck and, with a wink, hand me a Ding Dong out of his lunch pail as though it were the most prized possession in the world.

And let's face it. It was.

We weren't a Ding Dong family back then. If we didn't kill it, grow it, or obtain it in a five-gallon bucket at Costco or from the clearance shelves at the bread outlet, we didn't have it. So these moments in my grandpa's truck are some of my most cherished memories with him. I can still smell the chocolate as my tiny frozen fingers unfolded that shiny silver wrapper layer upon layer until I could taste the glorious mash-up of what must be some sort of plastic meets sugar-replacement concoction.

We ran wild and free back then, my brothers and I. There were ten kids within a few miles...all boys. And then there was me.

I ran with the pack the best I knew how, and *fear* wasn't a word we allowed to be tattooed on our hearts. As a mother, I tremble remembering the things we did when we were our kids' ages. My poor mom—if she only knew.

One of our favorite pastimes was a game my oldest brother dubbed "Timber" because when we weren't helping Grandpa eat his lunch or Dad plant trees, or finding licorice root to eat off tree trunks for survival purposes, we basically took on the form of the lost boys from *Peter Pan*. And as the only girl, I was the guinea pig for all of the boys' harebrained schemes.

So when my brother got this super fun idea that someone should climb to the top of the trees near the swamp, I was the one nominated. When the boys at the bottom decided it would be a fun idea to take an axe to the base of the tree, it was me who got the "opportunity" to find out what it feels like to fly. At least until I landed in the muddy swamp 20 feet below.

It's been two decades since those days in the woods with my own version of Neverland, and I still can't help but laugh every time I think about that story. I could learn so much from my younger self. The audacity, the stupidity, the bravery.

Sometimes I think we need to get a little more stupid about following God. *Webster* suggests the word *stupid* implies someone who goes through life making decisions that lack common sense. And I think God is all about things that lack common sense.

If God were into common sense, He wouldn't have birthed the Savior from a virgin, saved a nation through a murderer, flooded an earth that had never seen rain, or created a new order where the last is first and the first is last.

It doesn't make sense, right? So take heart. If God is asking you to do something that doesn't make any sense, you're in some seriously great company.

You know who I think would relate a bit to this? You know who I think would be our number one fan and would climb right up those trees with us, getting excited about falling into a swamp and doing something completely crazy and unconventional?

David. I think David would be all about something like that. David is one of my favorite Bible guys, and he was all about doing stupid things out of love. As a child, David walked right up to a man literally twice his size to battle against him for his people with a slingshot and five rocks. Does anything about that story make sense to you? Does any part of that bring peace to your heart? No one hears that and thinks, *Sure...everything is going to go great. David is going to come out just fine. Let's all go get our chairs so we can get good seats for this, because this is going to go down as one of the greatest underdog hero stories of all time!*

No! We aren't saying that at all, and neither were his people. Imagine living in David's village back then. Imagine being his *mother*!

Could you watch him take on a giant with a slingshot? Nope. That would not be a battle you'd want to see. If you're anything like me, you'd probably be hiding behind a tent making soup and waiting for someone to bring you news. But that's not how David rolled. Fear didn't own him the way it does so many of us.

I feel David and I will get along great in heaven. We are both a little nutty, love to dance, and are a little emotional (okay, maybe a lot emotional), and we've both made terribly bad decisions that got swallowed in God's grace. We both dive headfirst into crazy things God asks of us. I don't think I'd be as brave as David was in the Goliath situation, but when it comes to things not involving weapons, I'm all over jumping into crazy.

David isn't really a bury-his-shekels-in-the-sand kind of guy. And as someone who is called a man after God's own heart, I definitely think that spirit is something that should grab our attention and cause us to reflect a bit on our own lives.

Recently I was at a women's conference hosting a booth for the Adventures with Archer journals that I designed with my kids. I got into a conversation with a few moms who came to our table, and they asked me if it was hard to start making the books.

I remember hesitating and tilting my head at their question. I didn't quite understand what they were saying. "What do you mean?" I asked back.

"Well, it looks like a lot of work. Wasn't it hard to come up with all of this and get it going and ready for sale?"

I paused long enough to process whether or not I was going to be honest in my reply. I decided that since my face can't lie anyway, I'd better just be upfront with them. "Uh...nope," I said. "It wasn't hard at all. I barely even thought about it. We just had the idea, so we went with it. And now, here they are." The women cocked their heads, looked at me a little perplexed, and kept pressing me with questions.

Why do I FIGHT SO HARD against a SAVIOR who wants to WASH me WHITE like SNOW and COVER me in HIM?

For the first time in my entire adult life, I started to realize that blind jumping after God's promptings wasn't exactly a universally shared trait among Christians. Apparently this jump-then-think trait was a unique gift that God had woven deeply into my being. I could see their wheels turning, and looking back I wish I had asked them why they were so baffled by this concept. It made me wonder if God was pulling on their hearts about something, but they hadn't yet been brave enough to admit it to themselves or take it beyond the dream stage.

As a builder, my heart breaks at things like that. Simultaneously, I'm insanely curious. What is holding everyone back? More specifically— what is holding *you* back? Is there something that God has been whispering to your heart or continually bringing up in your life and asking you to step out in it?

What is He saying?

Why aren't you doing it?

What's keeping you from just following His lead?

I mean, He did create you. And He, more than anyone, knows not only what you are gifted at but also what is going to bring you the most joy and fulfillment and get you closer to who you are meant to be, right?

So what's with the pause? What is stopping you from taking just one tiny step in the direction of His invitation? I think now would be a great time to stop reading and write down what God has been pressing on your heart and what the obstacle is to taking a step toward it.

Go ahead. I'll wait.

_____

_____

_____

_____

_____

All of this reminds me of the men in Matthew 25 who were given talents to take care of while their master was away. Upon returning, the men to whom the master had given five and two talents had made good investments, and they were able to return to their master the original shekels plus what they had earned. When the master went to the man to whom he had given one talent, this was his response: "Master, I knew you to be a hard man, reaping where you did not sow, and gathering where you scattered no seed, so I was afraid, and I went and hid your talent in the ground. Here, you have what is yours" (ESV).

Ugh. There's that nasty word again. "I was *afraid*." Fear of disappointing his master was the obstacle that kept this man from making a good decision that would have led to blessing. Instead, it led him to his own demise. Sadly, this story is replaying itself every day in lives of probably thousands, if not millions, of hearts all over the world. People are choosing to succumb to fear and bury their gifts in the sand because they fear what will happen if they try to use them and mess up.

As a child, some of my favorite books involved alternate endings. The stories would play out, and along the way you could choose your own adventure. Each choice turned a different page in the story that ultimately gave way to a different ending for the character's life.

I don't know exactly why, or if everyone else did this too, but I couldn't help but go through the book multiple times, purposefully choosing a different answer each time to see what the outcome was.

I wanted to know all of the options.

And somehow that curiosity has stuck with me. I'm constantly playing out scenarios and making up endings for different situations in my own life and the lives of those around me.

So I'm curious. What about you? What's your alternative ending?

So much of fear is wrapped up in two tiny words...

What if?

What will happen if I step out...if I risk...if I fail?

What happens if I put it all out on the line and it doesn't go the way I had planned?

What if I do this, start this, move there, and I lose everything?
What if I end up having to move back, or start over, or quit my dream?
Those are good questions. But I have another one to ask.

One that I feel is gravely more important. Even eternally important.
What if you don't?

What would happen if you continued on with your life the way it's been going? What if you didn't take that job, move to that city, take that risk, start that business, make that phone call, create that product, or reach out to that person?

What would come of it? What would come of you?

What if you never paused long enough to write those words God has been blazing on your heart because you fear they'll never actually be published? Or if you never applied for that promotion because you were afraid you wouldn't get it? Or never moved to that city because you were afraid of starting over?

Dear friend, I want to flip the question in your mind. Stop asking what could go wrong, and start asking what could go right.

What good, amazing, incredible things could happen if you just stepped out?

What are the potential blessings? Opportunities? Relationships?

Write those down too.

What you focus on will drive you one way or another. It will drive you to step out, or it will drive you to stay put. And both are wise choices in their specific time. But for this story, I want to focus on whatever it is that God is tugging on your heart to do. If you focus on what could go wrong, the more you repeat those thoughts and delay action, the more rooted they become, until one day you wake up, and they are fruitful, strong, hearty trees of regret.

Yep, that's what I said. Because throughout my life, and from listening to countless stories from others' lives, I have seen that inaction is almost always followed by regret.

Following these promptings over the years has certainly cost me an immeasurable amount of grief. I've lost friends, money, businesses, opportunities. I have messed up more times than I can even account for. I've launched things that have fallen flat. Created things that never sold. And written things that were never good enough to publish.

But even after experiencing disappointment from the losses, the gains, successes, and victories shine brightly in comparison. I've realized that I'd much rather face the wreckage of stepping out than the regret of staying small.

> I'd much rather face the wreckage of stepping out than the regret of staying small.

I may be setting my sights too high in this regard, but a long time ago I made a pact with myself that I would live my life without regrets. I even shop this way. As a self-admitted non-shopper, I do realize that on occasion I have to make purchases to keep myself clothed. It's tragic, I know. But in this truth, I have found a very simplistic approach to filling my wardrobe. I simply ask myself, "Will I regret not purchasing this item?" If the answer is no, I won't regret stepping away and leaving the store without said item. On the contrary, if I feel in my heart— and I know we can all relate to this feeling—that I would get home, think about whatever the object is, and likely regret not buying it in the first place, then I save myself the inevitable grief of walking away by just buying the thing.

When it comes to my life in 50 years, I'd rather regret a step of faith I *did* make than one I never dared to make. Because if I dare to try something, if I step out, if I grab the hand of my ever-loving Father who is inviting me to join Him on an adventure, how could that ever lead to actual failure?

To me there is no such thing as failing, just learning.

And I'd so much rather spend my life living and learning than hiding my shekels because I'm more afraid of what could go wrong than what could go right.

So let's flip the question, friend. Let's not get to the end of all of this and face the regrets of things not done, stories not lived, and faith not stretched.

Let's start focusing on all that could go wonderfully right if we choose to step beyond whatever is holding us back, and follow God into something that doesn't make sense.

Let's be a generation that doesn't bury our shekels in the sand, but picks up a slingshot and some stones instead.

17

Your Choice

Success is liking yourself, liking what you do, and liking how you do it.

MAYA ANGELOU

It's strange how we treat ourselves in ways we would never treat someone else. Oftentimes we would tear someone else apart if they treated our loved ones the same way.

Yet somehow we are totally okay being completely terrible to ourselves. The expectations, the lies, the constant beating up of ourselves and comparing our shortcomings to other people's successes.

The other day I was reflecting on the beautiful sisters God has brought into my life. Two through my brothers and one through my husband. Each so vastly different from the other, but all beautiful, powerful, and purposeful in their own ways.

One of them is a stay-at-home mama who runs her business from her home. Another stays home with her three boys and leads a women's ministry at her church. The third works late-night nurse's shifts, juggling kid duties with my brother, who works at the sheriff's department.

As I was thinking about them, I was struck by the insane beauty and blessing we all have to create the lives we want around what matters the most to us. Yet with this freedom, we've somehow created a culture that celebrates others' lifestyles and discounts our own. What's good for her is no longer just good for her. Now it also equals good for her, bad for me.

I watch through the lenses of social media and get a chance to peek in on the lives of incredible women all over the world. Some are filling their days gathering chicken eggs and getting their hands dirty in the garden. Others are teachers, oilers, missionaries, speakers, knitters, homeschoolers, or students. Each one doing amazing things with what they've been given. Yet on occasion I struggle deeply with the fact that they have it all together, and thus, I must not. Their children are clean, or their cabinets are white, or they are saying something clever and encouraging while I can't even figure out which button makes the coffee turn on in the morning.

This round and round in my head nags me and makes me feel I must be doing something wrong because I'm not as color coordinated, well spoken, creative, or well connected as the pretty girl staring at me through my phone who obviously showered this morning while I tucked my hair in a messy bun and worked in my pajamas.

Running my own business just adds to the crazy. Throw three kids into the mix, and I can basically just commit myself right now. It's a *lot* to manage. And the constant swirling of thoughts that everyone must be doing it right except me makes the battle even fiercer...and my heart weaker.

Why do I do this to myself? Why do I let the lies win when I know that other women aren't the standard for my life or happiness? Why do I get down on myself whenever I see someone execute their business better than I do, or launch an idea before I can get around to it, or take a day off to go to the beach with their family when we haven't done that in months?

No matter what someone else is doing, or what kind of life they are living, it seems I can find a way to turn it into a lie that I am not measuring up. And worse, that I'm actually completely messing up at this whole life thing in general.

It reminds me of the scene in *Baby Mama* when Tina Fey's character,

Kate, is talking to Amy Poehler's character, Angie, who's Kate's surrogate mom. Angie's character is kind of a screw-up and seems to have believed a whole slew of lies about herself and her worth. Somewhere along the way she stopped thinking she could do anything differently than what she had learned was her normal. One day Kate says to her, "Angie, you can still have a completely different life."

That line always gets me. Like a slap in the face to wake up and realize we have entirely more control than we sometimes give ourselves credit for. It's so easy to get down on ourselves about the lives we live and the situations we find ourselves in. It's so easy to whine about what we don't have in the light of what everyone else seems to have. But we need to wake up and realize that these pity parties can actually kill our purpose. Getting down on ourselves about what we don't have and the lives we aren't living will actually build a higher fence between us and the lives we ultimately long for.

One thing I love so much about my sisters is how drastically different they are. And yet they all seem so fulfilled and at peace in the roles they've filled their lives with. It's a beautiful picture that puts to death the lie that "good for her means bad for me." It cuts the string that holds us in bondage to the lie that the only success that can ever be found is in "her" way of life, or "her" way of mothering, or "her" business model.

And who is this infamous "her" we are all chasing after in the first place?

Beauty and true fulfillment are found in the realization that my life doesn't have to look the same as anyone else's to be successful. That a successful, bright, beautiful, fully alive life can be built out of whatever I want to fill it with.

And no one is better at measuring what that looks like than I am.

And no one is a better compass to uncover it than Christ.

This is one of the most liberating things I've discovered in recent years—especially in the digital age of entrepreneurism. My days don't have to look like anyone else's in order to be successful or filled with deep purpose. And neither do my business, my kids, my marriage, my childcare situation, my days off, my vacation, or my income level.

When I fully embraced this truth, it was as if someone reached down and lifted the veil from my eyes and hundreds of bricks from my shoulders.

These lives of yours and mine are filled with thousands and thousands of choices. And we are the ones who get to seek God for direction, and then, we also get to choose. Sometimes a completely different life is but one choice away. Beyond all of the ways God leads us in our lives, there are also plenty of choices left to us. We've been given the gift to seek after Him, to follow His lead, and then to choose.

The Bible tells us how to love and how to live. It leads us in the way of forgiveness and walking righteously, but it doesn't lay out every single decision we will ever make. It doesn't tell us how much money we should make or what kind of job to do. It doesn't tell us to say yes to that opportunity or to pass it up. It doesn't tell us where to move, what to create, and whom to marry. We are blessed with the ability, and the freedom, to make choices.

Isn't that just the most beautiful, loving gift from our Father?

So this is where it really gets fun. We have the incredible blessing of deciding what success means for us and for our family in any given season. And the best part is the definition can change whenever we want.

Over the course of our marriage, success to me has taken on the forms of staying home with our newborn baby, homeschooling our son, juggling business and toddlers, and now settling into the rhythms of working only while the kids are in school.

And embracing this ebb and flow as the tides turn, and the seasons change, and the lines on the growth chart in the hall get higher and higher has been the most refreshing and restorative gift in my adult life.

I've had financial goals from making enough to take our family to Hawaii or to pay for private school all the way to saving enough to buy a vacation home or building an international family business.

As it stands right now, success for me involves a deep commitment to being present, and whole, and excitedly engaged with the people who mean the most to me.

It means working while my kids are in school and having the discipline to close my laptop and keep my phone in another room when they are home.

It means saying no to travel so I can say yes to chaperoning the field trip to the pumpkin patch or to teaching my daughter and her friends how to put on makeup.

It means taking a break from All. The. Sports. Commitments. So we can say yes to gathering around the table to truly connect as a family every single night. And just a little side-note: If you're an exhausted mama running your kids from one practice to another, throwing cheeseburgers at them from the front seat of your car, I feel you. That was us too.

Last year as I started planning for the weeks' meals I realized that we were only home maybe one night a week all together for dinner. We had cross-country practice from 3–5:30, and football from 5–7, and we spent all of our time in our car, divided by activities, and not connecting with our children, and there was no end in sight. As soon as these ended, basketball would start, and then baseball and track in the spring, giving us a three-week window before football started again in the fall.

Now, I *love* sports. I grew up an athlete, and I love the camaraderie, the discipline, and the team spirit, but the whole thing began to really wear on my mama heart, and I found myself praying that it would All. Just. Stop.

And then I remembered that we have a choice in all of this. I remembered that what we were allowing into the rhythms of our children's days were the building blocks of their childhood. This is what they will remember. And all too soon, our time to bring all of our little birds to the nest each night will be over.

So I stopped it.

We said we needed a break. To take some time off. And we stopped the cycle.

Because, friend, I was exhausted and so were they. We were all falling into not-good versions of ourselves because we were just so tired and overwhelmed. We were missing out on connecting with our kids. On laughing together. On just being us. And we weren't having family dinners anymore. Our family was slowly becoming what so many people talk about as two ships passing in the night in their marriages, but this was with our kids. And for what? So they could have more active lifestyles? So we could check off all of the boxes of proper kid experiences? I don't even know why. It just wasn't worth it for us. So we stopped.

We rewrote the rules for our family and decided that we would only commit to two team sports a year, and they couldn't be consecutive. I just can't handle six months straight of the madness. And you know what? The kids are happier too. At first I feared their sad hearts, or that they would feel left out, but it hasn't been that way at all. We do activities as a family, and we get out with each other. And even more importantly for us, we are connected. We are whole. We are laughing again. There isn't division, and crazy, and stress, and pressure, and rushing like there was before.

There is peace, and quiet, and time for conversations, and painting nails, and playing games, and gathering around the table.

And it's the best decision we have made in a long time.

But please remember...this is success to me and mine. This is what feels good and right and joy-filled for us in this season. If doing all of the sports for each of your kids means success to you, then by all means, do them. It's your choice. And it's okay to keep on keeping on, or to reevaluate and change the rules when you feel they need changing.

As each season, or goal, or dream changes, I have the freedom to just roll with it, and so do you. We get to believe and trust that God will fulfill His purposes in us as we continue to keep Him at the center, stay pliable to His promptings, and pick up, lay down, step out, or stop as He leads.

We've been given the GIFT to SEEK after GOD, follow HIS lead, and then, WE GET TO CHOOSE.

The best part of embracing this epiphany is the freedom found in a place that used to hold me captive. Now, instead of feeling less than, or outdone, or like I'm missing out or falling behind when I see another woman succeeding at her dreams or running her family a certain way, I experience a genuine celebration dance going on inside my heart.

Because she has found her own way, and I've found mine.

And that's just the best of both worlds.

18

Make It Plain

Where there is no vision, the people perish.

PROVERBS 29:18 KJV

As our family started going on vision retreats and paying attention to the threads that tie us together, we've discovered something alarming, and breathtakingly beautiful. We found that our whole family has a similar heartbeat that just takes on different roles. It's almost like that of an orchestra, all instruments working together for the same melody, each with different and necessary parts and sounds, some similar, some opposite.

But we never would have noticed had we not written our dreams and passions down, and taken some time to mull them over. It reminds me of the verse in Habakkuk 2:2 where God tells Habakkuk to "write the vision; make it plain" (ESV). Although I don't know the exact interpretation of this verse, and I'm not sure if writing down a vision for your life is what it actually means, I do find it interesting that God goes on to say, "so that others may run with it." And that seems like pretty spot-on advice to me.

Something we've learned through intentionally seeking God together for our family's vision is to move forward only in unity. God is a God of unity, and if you seek Him, He won't lead you and your spouse in different directions. So if you're not on the same page about a decision, stop. Do not move ahead without unity.

Moving forward with something when there is division is laying the foundation for an "I told you so" conversation later. So we just don't do that anymore.

If you aren't in unity on something, keep praying. Keep laying down your own desires and picking up God's. Keep leaning in. Keep listening. Keep writing down your dreams and visions, and looking for common threads. And wait until pattern and unity reveal themselves. Once you have unity, you have a solid foundation to move forward.

As we continued to write things down, we discovered that despite being so different, we all have very specific passions that build well upon each other.

Here are some of our findings: I am a dreamer. (Shocker.) And a builder. A connector of hearts and igniter of possibility. I adore village living and live for family dinners and rooms full of people laughing and sharing stories late into the night. I feel most alive when I can help others live free and loved, and help them move past whatever hurts have come their way.

And you know what? My whole family feels this way too. In all different ways.

While I dream of owning a farm with patio lights strung high from trees, decorating beautiful dinner parties for people, and collecting chicken eggs to give away, my family has dreams that intertwine with mine. Ava, our oldest, dreams of baking, and coffee shops, and selling her art in a cute little shop. Isaiah, our ten-year-old, can't stop talking about the animals we will have and what we will serve for breakfast at the bakery. He talks about big trucks, working the farm, and setting up community movie nights on the side of the barn.

And Isaac, my favorite human, just wants to serve everyone. Me, the kids, the community, people who visit the farm. He's amazing. And it makes him shine his absolute brightest when he gets to serve. I promise I can see the whole thing playing out as if we were actually already living it. He wants to keep up the land, run a coffee shop, manage the properties, and learn how to make things with his hands and piles of wood, just like my grandpa did.

As we continued to write down all the things and prayed about them over the past several years, God began to refine our vision and create a clear path in our minds.

We started to see more than a farm just for our family. We saw a haven, a safe place, a land of community, and connection, and family, and belonging. We saw a ministry farm retreat center. Haven Hill Farm, to be exact.

A place for others to call home and awaken adventure.

As we began to heal and experience more of the joy, freedom, and restoration God had for us, we also began to feel a tremendous burden and unbridled passion to help others find their way out of the woods and into the freedom found in the Father's heart.

New dreams were birthed for this property we'd held in our hearts for so long. And we found ourselves planning, praying, and pondering the possibilities during most of our waking hours. "What if we could create a space for couples, and families, and leaders, and authors to return to rest and connect with the heart of God? A place to heal, experience new adventures, soak in community, rest in God, and laugh again. What if we could build a safe haven for them?" we began to say "A luxurious, peaceful retreat to come to with their spouses, or their kids, or to be alone with their thoughts and dreams. A place of connection, and hope, and grace, and community, and adventure.

"A place to commune with God, and community, and fill days with long meals, kayaking, tending animals, mountain climbing, or reading in a hammock. A place we wished we could have found when we were down and out, on the brink of destruction, divorce, and isolated depression, but couldn't.

"What if we could make a place like that?"

During these dream sessions, our farm took on a whole new life, and God began laying very specific things on our hearts. We will build ten cabins, each with two rooms and a living area, sleeping eight to ten people. They will be comfortable enough for two couples or a family with children to make themselves at home for a weekend, a month—whatever they needed. We will have a few Airstreams about the property for people looking for solitude, writing a book, or needing time with their thoughts. The farm will ideally be 100 acres, but no less than 60. On another part of the property we will build two or three houses for our host families.

We will work together to keep up the farm, love the guests, and cultivate an environment of grace, hope, connection, and fully alive hearts. A community barn will be in the middle of the place. We will gather there often for music, dancing, painting, or even paintball. It will act as a gathering space for guests and visitors, as well as an event center for the farm and local community. We can imagine having worship nights in the barn and showing old movies on the side of it in the summer. We can see huge community gatherings for the local city. We will live, fully alive, for a cause greater than ourselves.

The guest cottages will be a safe haven for people who have experienced trauma in some way and are just trying to find their way home again. It will be for those who've been lied to, or hurt, or have lost something great, and are just trying to find who God really is again. It will be for the couples who have lost the passion they once held dear, and the artist who needs space to be, and process, and create. It will welcome the pastors who are tired, and the burned-out people who need to be inspired, and the orphans who've finally found family in someone's arms.

The farm will be for the people who need quiet and laughter, love and truth...and who most of all need a family to give their legs the strength to hold them up again.

Maybe they will come for a weekend, or maybe a few months, but we will love on them, and stand by them, and basically be to them what we needed someone to be for us these past few years. Because I truly believe that our pain gives birth to our purpose. And our cries teach us how to respond to the cries of others.

Most of all we see home, and belonging.

A place where love wins and failures fall in the light of His glory. We see redemption, and wholeness, and laughter. We see purposes unveiled, families restored, and hearts coming alive.

And as with everything we've lived for, we see this farm as a place where women, and families, and marriages can uncover the heart of God for their lives and walk in the fullness of their calling. Where passions can be birthed and gifts brought to life.

A place where joy, and adventure, and laughter, and story are thickly woven into our fabric.

We see it as the heart of our ministry that lived online for so many years taking on tangible form. A place where we can meet people face-to-face every day—serving them, loving them, equipping them, and unleashing them into their fullest and freest selves. A place where we can wash people in the love and grace of God, and see their hearts and relationships burst forth in new freedom and passion.

There will be chickens and goats, and hopefully an English mastiff puppy. Or two.

We will smile.

And laugh.

And we will feel Alive.

And Free.

And Purposeful.

And at Peace...

This is our family's vision.

And now that it's written out, it seems so clear. So possible. We don't know how, but we are believing that somehow, in a way only God can do, He will bring us a property to build the farm on. And He will bring along people and families to link arms with us to make it happen.

We aren't about to try to guess how this will all happen, but I do know that God has put this vision on our hearts, brought us into unity, and prompted us to write it down for a reason. So I think it's safe to assume He has something up His sleeve.

When we allow the LOVES of our HEARTS to be WASHED AWAY by the BUSY we SIMULTANEOUSLY turn down the VOLUME of GOD'S voice in our lives.

I firmly believe that as much as I fought staying in Oregon, surrounded by these wet forests, God is about to show up in this state in bigger ways than I can fathom. I believe there is rest, and peace, and *selah* in the mountains He crafted here, and that the people needing this space to call home actually need it to be remote and uncharted. I believe there is so much magic in going off the beaten path. And I'm so thankful that is where God is calling us.

God, please work. Please move. Please complete the good work You have started in our family. Please don't delay…let everything here be my prayer to You. And change my heart if these don't line up with Your will.

Move, Jesus. Please. My heart is heavy and weary. I need to see You part the seas in my life. And move mountains in my story.

———

If you, like me, have things swirling in your head…

If you don't name your dreams out loud, but they still won't go away…

If you've longed for clarity…

If people keep asking you *what you really want*, give yourself this gift:

Here, today, write the vision and make it plain. Draw a mark in the sand saying that today you are believing for these things that you know God has put things on your heart on purpose. For a purpose.

Then let's sit on the edge of our seats together and watch God move.

legacy

*Please think about your legacy, because
you're writing it every day.*

GARY VAYNERCHUK

I opened the door and made my way out to the hallway where guests were being welcomed. Ava stood there, eleven years old, tall and beautiful, with a stack of programs in her hand. She was strong, and brave, and ready to be a friendly face on a somber day. Just beyond her and outside, I watched in awe as person after person made their way to greet my grandma. The line felt miles long, and kept growing. I'd never seen anything like it. As soon as some people were welcomed inside, others appeared at the back of the line outside to fill in the gaps.

My family filed into the front row and got as comfy as they could on the cold wooden pews. I couldn't join them. I just couldn't bear to. I stood back, watching, waiting, letting the magnitude of it all wash over me like poetry. I could see the entire church from where I stood swaying and soothing a sleeping babe in my arms.

Pew upon pew filled with friends of old and family overflowing. As I soaked it all in, a deep conviction fell upon my heart from what was unfolding. With more of Grandpa's family on the other side of eternity than on this one, this little church was still filled to the brim with lives changed by his goodness and love.

As we sang hymns and told stories, I was struck by the impact of a life lived out in simple, everyday love. The kind that our parents grew up with and Andy Griffith talked to Opie about. My heart became burdened with the fast-paced society we call home, and the depravity of the "what's next," "if your dream doesn't scare you, it's not big enough," "hustle 'til it hurts" movements.

The pastor stood in front of a communion table my grandpa built with his bare hands and began to speak. He talked about how Grandpa just showed up places. He recounted coming home to find Grandpa rototilling the parsonage yard to help prepare the ground for a garden. He told stories of the years and years my grandpa spent showing up and mowing the church's lawn without ever being asked.

Grandpa spent his whole life showing up for people, and on that sunny day in October, they all showed up for him.

I didn't say much that day, or the rest of the week, for that matter. I just kept envisioning the line of people that extended down the church steps and into the parking lot. Face upon face, life upon life, opportunity upon opportunity that Grandpa seized to show love in one more way.

I imagine that heaven probably had a very similar scene that week. Except instead of the line of people walking toward my grandma offering hugs and condolences, it was a crowd of those who'd gone before him lining up to welcome Grandpa home.

The passing of a life can hit us like a raindrop of information or an ocean of emotion. One causes us to pause, think for a moment, and quickly move on, while the other leaves an uncontrollable current of memories, surges of laughter, aching tears, and cries that burst forth, causing our entire bodies to shake and our bellies to groan—all depending on the relationship we had with the life gone before us.

The following weeks were a dance of anger, tears, tiny smiles, and introspection. I just kept seeing the faces, and I couldn't shake them. As they stared back at me in my mind's eye, I began to wonder, *What faces would show up for me?*

Would anyone care?

Would anyone come?

I wish I could say that I have poured so much love, and community, and servant-hearted hospitality into my world that I quickly envisioned a similar line at my funeral. But the life I had been living didn't feel deserving of a standing-room-only celebration into heaven. It more accurately lined up with a table for ten filled with our extended family, and maybe, maybe, a few friends from Bible study.

The hours I spent in the church that day, prepping for Grandpa's service and hugging all the guests until the hall was empty, felt like a call home. It was an invitation into a life I had been too busy to notice.

My own.

Running an online business and leading an international women's ministry are beyond amazing experiences. I find my heart gleaming with gratitude at the mere thought God would entrust me with such things. But amid the drive and dedication, the striving and social media, I suddenly realized I was missing the very best thing.

My actual own life.

At times it can feel as if I live in two worlds. My work life, and the one surrounded by grazing horses and giggling children. Both wonderful. Both important. Both needed. But somewhere along the path, I'd opened the doors of my heart to feel burdened by family and exhilarated by productivity.

I don't know if it was the accolades, the buzz of creativity, or the fact that I finally got to dress up in grown-up clothes, free of peanut butter fingerprints, and participate in an inspiring conversation. Whatever it was, it snuck in undetected for years and almost got away with stealing away the very best pieces of my heart, the ones that come alive in this place I call home.

I felt as if I were the only woman on earth torn between two loves like this. And the guilt almost ripped me in two. But as I started sharing my story with others, something phenomenal began to unravel. A pattern. Turns out it wasn't just me. Stories from the lives of women all around me began to echo in my heart. Stay-at-home moms who felt torn by ministry opportunities or volunteering in their kids' class-rooms. Students who loved learning and traditional education but also longed to take off and explore the world. The office worker who dreams of opening an art studio, or building a home and family.

As it turns out, we all have our things. We all have the stuff that fills our hearts and the stuff that fills our days. We just need to figure out how to make it all work together. Like my grandpa did. His love for building, creating, and helping didn't take him out of his life; it grounded him more deeply in it. And I think that's what we are all seeking to find in this wild goose chase after all. A way to fill our days with the stuff that fills our hearts.

There's a deeply rooted yearning in all of us, I think, to be a part of something bigger than us. Something that matters. Something that will go on long after we are gone and make a difference. But somehow, in an instant, as the pastor spoke, and stories were told, and wrinkled cheeks brushed each other in long hugs, it all began to make a little more sense.

> What if this huge, magnificent impact I dream of making isn't something I accomplish, or build, or do? What if it's who I show up for? Who I serve? Who I love?

What if this bigger thing I've been searching for has been right here all along?

What if this thing that matters, and will live on long after I'm gone, is right in front of me? Staring back at me through the eyes of those who share my days, and my bathroom, and my table? What if this huge, magnificent impact I dream of making isn't something I accomplish, or build, or do? What if it's who I show up for? Who I serve? Who I love?

We all have these convictions, don't we? These things we wish the world would become. The things we want to stand for, tattoo on our arm, and pray our neighborhoods will turn into. But what if we are a bigger part of making these changes than we realize? What if God meant what He said when He told us to love our neighbor as ourselves?

Is that really what we are doing? What I am doing? Or have I been so busy building bigger, dreaming larger, and encouraging the already encouraged that I've missed the whole point?

I can still picture walking to school past the parsonage building as a teenager, waving to my grandpa as he pushed the mower. His hands dirty with the smearing of soil. His smile creased from age but brighter than ever. I must have done this a hundred times throughout my high school years, and I never gave it a second thought.

But that day in October, pictures of him with his mower, and his jigsaw, and his shovel filled my every thought. Ninety-one bells began to ring from the old church steeple. The same steeple he and Grandma were married under 67 years ago and my mom was baptized in.

Tears started to rise up, and I struggled to hold them back.

The room was silent. Uncomfortable. Everyone stared blankly in different directions as we were all forced to listen and be still.

Ding.

Ding.

Ding...

One year. Two years. Three...

No one said a word, but they didn't have to. I knew what they were all thinking. Every one of them had been touched by the sincere heart and servant's hands of my favorite grandpa. He never did anything fancy, or huge, or earth shattering. What he did was better than all of that. Because he loved as Jesus did. With availability, and presence, and showing up for people using the gifts he had to offer.

I began to realize that he didn't have to change the whole world because he changed my whole world. And on that crisp, sunny fall day, I sat among a few hundred people who felt the same way. Each one changed forever by the love of a man carrying a saw, a shovel, and a smile.

His life was proof that the lies we tell ourselves don't actually carry the weight we give them. The ones that say, "There is nothing special about you," "You don't have anything to offer." The lies that ask us,

"Who would really want what you could give?" He squashed all of those lies when he chose to use the seemingly insignificant things he did well as an offering to those around him.

He broke the mold and brought truth to those whispers with the testimony of a life well lived, a family well loved, and a community well served.

> Legacies aren't built around one big change or grand gesture. They are built brick by brick, over time, with one little act, one little word, one little smile.

I can't help but wonder what people will say of me one day, and I think it's wise to give it some time to mull over. We never know how life will play out or when our time will run out. If we want to leave a legacy, we must live the life we want to be remembered for now.

We must do it today.

And then again tomorrow.

For legacies aren't built around one big change or grand gesture. They are built brick by brick, over time, with one little act, one little word, one little smile.

It's been months now since his service, and I wonder what I have in my toolbox that I can use to love like he did. What passions do I carry that I can bring home? Or next door? Or to the kids' school? And maybe you should start wondering too. How can we overflow our unique talents and bring them into our everyday? To our kids? To our homes? To our communities?

What gifts do we all carry that we may have thought were limited to our jobs, or ministries, or committees that could change our whole worlds if we simply redirected and duplicated them?

When I left the church that day, I felt a fire ignited in my soul to start remembering who I was before all of the jobs, and titles, and accolades. To start cultivating who I was created to be for Ava, and Isaiah, and Logan, and my amazing hunk of a husband, Isaac. Who was I created to be for them? More than just filling their bellies and folding their clothes, what is my part of their story? What am I supposed to say? What gifts am I supposed to encourage? What conversations am I supposed to have? What am I supposed to show them through my actions toward them and the words I speak? What dreams of theirs am I supposed to support?

What tools do I have in my toolbox that are meant to help them build their path?

What tools do you have in yours?

The questions swirled like wildfire. Picking up more strength as I gave them more fuel. And soon it all became convictingly clear. More than those I serve in my work, I want to be a stepping-stone in the lives God has put in front of me. I want to fill my todays with experiences and adventures that will make tomorrow's memories a happy story, not a heartbreaking one.

I want to live a life worthy of a standing-room-only service and a wake of stories.

Because it really is true: "The passing of a life can hit us like a raindrop of information or an ocean of emotion."

And I want to leave an ocean.

PART 3

Presence

There's magic in WAKING UP, rediscovering OUR WAY, and GETTING LOST in the things that used to KEEP US UP at night.

Return to Me

Don't let other people decide who you are.

BOB GOFF

I stepped onto the mat and started drying off from my toes up. The bath is my happiest of places. The warmth. The silence. It's like soaking in a hug from my Savior and giving my body and mind space to finally pause and take a breath.

There are no tasks in the bathtub—just soaking, and silence, and pondering, and planning. We don't have a tub at our home right now, so whenever I travel for work, I always book the room with the nicest bathroom…and I hope, a huge bathtub.

This time I was in a lodge just outside of Nashville with a small leadership team. As I dried off, I heard something that jolted me, but not in an abrasive way. More like an unexpected invitation way. I paused as the lyrics of one of my favorite singers filled the air and instantly took me back 15 years.

Something foreign and distant, yet familiar and true. As I followed the sound into the other room, the words and melodies echoed through the air, and it felt as if I was stepping into my own skin again.

Like I had finally made my way home.

I stood for several minutes just listening and drinking it in. *Why is this so weird?* I wondered. This used to be my everyday rhythm. This

167

used to be me. And now that I thought of it, it used to be Isaac and me too. Together.

So why did this feel so different? Why was something that used to be as comfortable as my favorite worn-in blue hoodie suddenly feeling so foreign? So strange?

As I continued to get closer to the music, the strong, smooth tone of Tim McGraw's voice embraced me like the welcomed hug of a loved one seen after years apart. Suddenly I realized why this whole situation was so haunting. *I don't listen to country music anymore,* I thought. *Actually, I haven't listened to country music in years.*

The realization was almost paralyzing as I stopped to ponder the situation.

How on earth did this happen?

Why?

When?

How had the music that was the anthem of my childhood and the soundtrack of Isaac and me falling in love under the Texas sky become completely nonexistent in my life?

Where did it go? Why had it gone away?

I sat on the bed in complete disbelief. And a bit of sorrow. I couldn't understand how something that I loved so much had simply disappeared. It dawned on me that somewhere along the way, the opinions of people around me and the voices of those who lived within my walls had somehow stripped me of my own.

In 16 years of marriage, and 12 of motherhood, the giving, wiping, cooking, making, cleaning, hugging, teaching, and reading to the rhythm of everyone else's needs had somehow silenced my own.

Don't worry, friend. I'm not going to start rambling about self-care; that's a tangent for another day. But I do think it's important to consider another topic that may have been forsaken...being self-aware. I think it's safe to say that my revelation of a love long forgotten isn't an isolated case.

There's this
DEEP ACHE
in all of us
to know
We Are SAFE,
and HEARD,
and HELD.

As mamas, and wives, and daughters, and sisters, and friends, and creatives, it's so easy to spend our entire lives answering the needs of everyone around us, only to find ourselves years later, alone in a room, wrapped in a towel, with tears streaming down our face as we remember pieces of ourselves that somehow disappeared along the way.

Trust me, I know this seems super trivial, but God can use seemingly insignificant things to wake us up to what is eternally significant. If I had let something so dear to my heart fade away over time, what else had God woven into my being that I'd let the busyness of life or the needs of others hush silent?

It seems to me that allowing the loves of our hearts to be washed away by the busy can somehow turn down the volume of God's voice in our life. Or at least the volume in which we are able to hear it. But when we are filling our days with the things that light our hearts on fire and feel authentic to our own souls, it creates an atmosphere where we can hear God more easily.

Have you ever found that to be true? Are there places you go, or things you do, or music you listen to that wakes up your insides and makes you feel more connected to God? Is it easier to hear God in those spaces?

It sure seems to ring true in our family. Our oldest daughter, Ava, feels more connected when she is painting, or baking, or playing the piano. While our middle son feels more alive and close to God when he's adventuring outside, running wild and unhindered. For my husband, the closeness happens in the mountains or when he gets to serve others. For me it's a warm bath, a quiet beach, a walk around our property, or the sounds of '90s country music filling my home while I cook dinner.

When I'm in these spaces, with these sounds, I'm flourishing in the best parts of who I am. My stresses are silenced, my worries fall to the wayside, and my heart feels open to receive what God has for me.

We all have these things, I think. Locations, lyrics, and loves that make us who we are and help us find the path we are supposed to walk down.

> In his grace, God has given us different gifts for doing certain things well. So if God has given you the ability to prophesy, speak out with as much faith as God has given you. If your gift is serving others, serve them well. If you are a teacher, teach well. If your gift is to encourage others, be encouraging. If it is giving, give generously. If God has given you leadership ability, take the responsibility seriously. And if you have a gift for showing kindness to others, do it gladly (Romans 12:6-8 NLT).

It's these unique gifts and passions that pave the way for our purpose. Someway, somehow, I believe all of these bents of ours are integral pieces of our bigger story, woven together in ways only God can do. And if we neglect the little pieces that make us come alive, I think that over time, the bigger passions, and the things we know we were made to do, will start to fade too.

Since my post–bubble bath epiphany in Nashville, I have made it a point to start listening to more of my favorite old country music. It may seem insignificant or even dumb, and I get that. But there's something magical about reconnecting with bits of yourself long silenced that can rekindle your insides and prepare you for what's next. And my hubby, in the sweetest of ways, has joined the party too. It's not a rarity for him to come up behind me in the kitchen, grab my hand, and pull me into a full dance right there by whatever is simmering on the stove.

We sway, and kiss, and get all caught up in each other again until a kid wraps us in their hug and starts to dance too. But the sweetness hasn't ended there. Strangely, and very unexpectedly, this new rhythm of mine, in the oddest of ways, has changed almost everything. My creativity has been ignited, and my path has become clearer. With less stress and more joy in my surroundings, I've been able to see what I need to be doing more of, and what I should take off my plate and do less of.

I've thought of new ideas and become more intentional with old ones. My yesses and nos are said with more purpose. More certainty. And somehow, almost unexplainably so, there is more laughter within our walls too. Maybe because it feels as though I've returned to myself again. And there's so much freedom in that. So much rightness.

It seems silly that playing different music during the day has led to such monumental change in our home. But, friend, I can't make this stuff up. I know there isn't magic in Tim McGraw's songs. Well, to me there is, but that's beside the point. What I have found more powerful is that there is a certain magic in returning to the pieces of us we once loved and somehow lost along the way.

When we shed the busyness of unending tasks to study the beauty of our unique souls, we'll find pieces of our purpose awaken. And glimpses of the Father we may have never noticed before.

There's magic in planting tulips, taking a dance class, sitting down to play the piano again, hitting a yard sale, or picking up that camera you boxed up years ago. There's magic in watering the seeds in our souls that were sown there by our Father who knows what's best for us and made us that way with great intention.

What dusty, forgotten things of yourself could hold life-altering magic for you? What would happen if you took time for them again? How would you feel? What possibilities could unfold if you took the steps to uncover your truest self? What legacy could you change?

I fully believe that the invitation to our destiny is ingrained in our desires. There's magic in waking up, rediscovering our way, and getting lost in the things that used to keep us up at night.

There's magic there, because that's where we can hear God the clearest. At least I've found that in my own life. When we shed the busyness of unending tasks to study the beauty of our unique souls, we'll find pieces of our purpose awaken. And glimpses of the Father we may have never noticed before.

When the striving is silenced, and we confidently settle into who we are truly created to be, we can finally hear the Voice that's been trying to get our attention all this time.

And I think we should start listening.

21

Culture of Home

What begins in the home stretches into eternity.

SALLY CLARKSON

I walked in and spotted the orange-brown tree house fort at the back of the store. It has been calling me, year after year, for more than a decade. I've always wanted to bring it home, and yet I never can. Last summer as we paid off our last bills and closed the sale on our house to buy some property in the country, I remember grinning ear to ear, thinking, *Next summer will be my summer. Next summer will finally be the year I get to bring the tree house home.*

We had done so well with downsizing over the past few years. We made really hard choices and lived in a teeny fixer-upper while we paid down bills. I'd wanted to get this tree house since the first summer Ava could walk, and I couldn't believe that after ten years of waiting, it would finally be mine. Even though we had missed the young years of our oldest kids, God had brought us a new babe, and hopefully he would grow to love it as I had always dreamed my children would.

As I walked toward the back of the store, being sure to go down every aisle of the gardening and outdoor play section, I got up close. This year there was something new, a twisty tube slide. It's my favorite kind of slide, as I don't have to worry about children jumping from the top of it or pushing each other out.

And this year it was only $999 dollars. I couldn't believe it. That was the cheapest one I had ever seen. Usually they were well over $1,000 and sometimes even $1,500. I was filled with the glimmer of hope that maybe this year could be it. Maybe this year we could finally bring it home to our kids.

As I took a photo and turned to walk away, my eyes filled with tears. I choked them back in disbelief that I was getting misty about a play structure and just kept walking. I made my way outside and pushed my cart to the car. It was my daughter's birthday. She was turning eleven. I opened the back of the car and turned to the cart where I gathered up two rotisserie chickens and a carton of croissants I had bought. It totaled $19.99. Probably the cheapest meal you could possibly find to feed 11 people. And nothing like the birthday dinner I had imagined and planned for her just weeks before. This was supposed to be our summer, remember? Our year of financial freedom.

We had just spent two solid, hard years in 1,000 square feet with five people, paying off debt, being responsible, and saying no to every extra expense. Yet, because I had misread a contract from the conferences we run, here I was again. Under the weight of so much business debt, I could barely breathe. Because of my mistakes, we could barely afford two whole chickens for my daughter's birthday party. And I was having to say no to my beloved tree house again, for the tenth year in a row.

Tears started to well up again, and I began to ask myself, "Why on earth is that tree house so important to me? Why do I have this decade-long obsession with this wooden Costco wonderland?"

And then, as quickly as the question came, so did the answer. I immediately heard the voice of my Father on my heart. "It's the only place you ever felt safe. It's the only place you ever felt home." Instantly I flashed back to my own 11-year-old self, watching the sunset over the mountains from the top of our cedar trees behind my house. I would go up there all the time back then. To a land my brothers and I constructed of tree forts, and cat walks, and rope ladders that would make even Ewoks jealous. I'd go there to escape. To think. To process and dream. But mainly to get away from the tension that lived inside the walls of our home.

In an instant, with one thought from His heart, it all made sense. I wasn't trying to buy my kids a tree house. I was trying to buy myself one.

My 34-year-old self, decades after my childhood, was longing for a tiny space high above the ground where I could be alone with my Father.

And maybe my kids would learn to meet Him there too.

This sense of home, and safety, and roots had almost been a god to me over the years. Something I clung to because clinging to people was too fragile, too risky. And clinging to God, well, I wasn't too sure about Him most days either during that season.

As I reflected back on my times in the trees, my heart immediately returned to Adam, a boy I'd known from birth who was more brother than neighbor. He was the right arm of my actual older brother, Luke. He caught the first piece of my childhood heart with his twinkling blue eyes, blond hair that fell across his forehead, and contagious smile.

As a new fifth grader in the vast sea of towering eighth graders, Adam's nod and beaming smile as we passed in the hall always made me feel safe again—just as he had my whole life. He and Luke had a way about them that just said, "Everything will be okay. I've got your back, and I'm not going anywhere." It's the way every girl needs to feel growing up, but it's the lucky ones who actually do.

I remember walking between my brother and Adam in the halls of my school and feeling like the queen of the world. With them I was untouchable, invincible. And safe. Always safe.

It had been like this my whole life until one afternoon in September when my whole world shattered to pieces. That afternoon, a typical after-school football practice became a turning point of my childhood, a scar on my family, and a prickly point between God and me that He's still teaching me how to make smooth again.

Adam collapsed on the football field that day in front of my brother Luke and the entire eighth-grade team. His jersey, #44, was cut off as people came to his aid, and he was rushed off in an ambulance. Luke returned home early and told us the news. I remember my little brother, Cody, leaving the room and reentering with his hand on the Bible. "Maybe this can help," he said in his sweet eight-year-old voice.

"That is not going to help," I foolishly whipped back at him. My words cut with the tone of an unapproving tween girl, and I could almost visibly see his hope diminish. To this day, saying those words is one of the deepest regrets of my entire life. My heart sank further, and although I instantly wanted to take back what I had just snapped out, I was simultaneously paralyzed with the fear that maybe, possibly, I was actually right. That God wasn't going to come through in the way we wanted after all.

Believing nothing I could say or do could take back what I already had done, I decided to say nothing more. We all just sat there, silent, dealing with our own doubts, fears, and disbeliefs in our own ways.

It felt like eternity as we waited for an update. I can still picture the scene as if I actually had a photograph of it. I can feel the tension. The fear. All of us staring at the floor. Luke pacing in the hall. Cody sitting there silently holding his Bible and hanging his head. I can still hear the knock on our door and the sound of the teammates' voices passing on the news that Adam was gone.

My whole family sank into a dark cloud of sadness. Luke first. Then the rest of us. We collapsed into grief, and then unbelief, and then back again. That afternoon my naïve young heart stepped out of a childhood I could never return to, and stepped into the reality that the world isn't always good, and things don't always go the way we want.

Simultaneously, it planted a seed in my ten-year-old soul that God was good to everyone else. He answered others' prayers. He came through for them. But me? My prayers? They simply weren't worth enough to catch His attention.

I started spending a lot of time in the trees after that. In quiet. In deep questioning. The same trees that we had played in with Adam now held a different emotion. Unquenchable pain. Whenever things in my adolescent heart would become too much to bear, I found myself walking out back, climbing up 30 feet of branches, and sitting among the treetops watching the sun set over the hills.

If I could venture a guess, I'd say that all of us are somehow trying to make our way back to our own version of the treetops. We all have them. The spaces that have held our tears and brought safety to our hearts and belonging to our souls.

Maybe it's a certain coffee shop you always go to, or a closet, or a car. Maybe it's not a place at all, and you find your solace in a brownie or a bottle. Or possibly both. However it unfolds for you, there's this deep ache in all of us to know we are safe, and heard, and held. And if we don't feel like Jesus is that place for us, we will search it out however we can, trying to heal the hurts with anything that will bring relief. Even if it's just for a minute.

This same heart cry has paved the way for me to be so intentional with the culture of our home as an adult. If others don't feel that they can go to God directly, I want to provide a place of peace so they can rest here. And hopefully, prayerfully, He will meet them while they are here. Just as He has with me.

This mission of providing solace and safety has given me a plumb line to help define what we stand for within our walls, and what we strive to keep out of them. I want to welcome questions and allow those who are here to wrestle with God on their own and know they are still loved. Still safe.

Above all, I want our home to stand for safety and belonging. I want all who enter to be bombarded with peace, and understanding, and prayer. And more than likely, a home-cooked meal that fills more than their bellies.

All of this, ironically, was unfolding in my heart as I made my way through the aisles of my favorite grocery warehouse. As I walked outside and started wiping the tears from my face, the Lord began to fill me with an urgency to make invitation my anthem.

Just as He had with us.

Jesus loved with INVITATION, not OBLIGATION. He provides safety, and acceptance, and LOVE for ALL of US to fall into and find the PIECES we NEED to get BACK UP again.

We all have our battles. And more than likely we will all find ourselves wrestling with God at some point or another as broken dreams and unanswered prayers crash their way into our lives. And it's important that we all have a safe place to land, and cry, and fight through it when we do.

He reminded me that Jesus loved with invitation, not obligation. He provides safety, and acceptance, and love for all of us to fall into and find the pieces we need to get back up again. And now He was inviting me be an extension of His great love for people. To use my home as His healing room. And my family as His face to a world searching for hope.

He invited me to be an inviter.

And asked me to use my welcome mat as our new mission.

And I can't wait to see who He'll bring through our door.

22

James

*God is more interested in your character than your comfort, and
he's more concerned about your holiness than your happiness.*

RICK WARREN

I've always been a big-dog person. Huge dogs, really. In the land of towering evergreen trees and steel cases full of hunting weapons, we were always taught that dogs had to serve a purpose or they weren't worth having.

I grew up with a mess of dogs all trained specifically for retrieving fallen birds in fields full of tall grass and marshlands. And although I didn't exactly inherit the hunting gene, I do carry with me a fascination for big, lovable puppies.

So when it came time for us to add a pup to our family, I did what any normal (okay, obsessive) adult would do. I perused the Internet for hours on end discovering everything there was to know about these four-legged, furry friends. After multiple dog-matching personality tests, I found myself face-to-face with the cutest, ugliest, largest animal baby I had ever seen.

I was smitten. His big, droopy eyeballs and gentle-giant personality had me at hello. And I knew instantly I was having my very own Jerry McGuire moment with my newest love. The English mastiff.

I've always been a jump-and-*then*-think type of person. So this sudden intrigue turned extreme obsession didn't catch me off guard.

However, all of my oohing and aahing over this elegant, giant crea-
ture seemed to be lost on my family. I was certain they would love this
majestic fur baby as much as I did, but oddly, his pictures didn't seem
to capture their attention at all.

You'd think this would have been a sign, and in hindsight, I wish it
had been. But I can get insanely tunnel-visioned when I want something. (I'm working on it, I promise.) But if things make sense to me,
it's hard for me to stop until I've persuaded everyone else around me
that what I am desiring to do is the absolute best decision we can make.
In this extreme commitment, I hold to my ideals. It may seem as if
I'm nagging or controlling, but that's not the case. At least, not exactly.

It's more like this: I discover something. I get excited. I talk about
it constantly and subscribe to multiple websites to ensure a constant
stream of this topic invades my inbox. My people, over time, are worn
down. Not by nagging, but by the simple fact that my behavior is
pretty insane, and they really just want me to stop talking about whatever it is I'm obsessing over.

So they cave.

The old me would have been super pumped about this result. I
would have felt some twisted victory knowing that I had turned their
perspectives and shown them the light. But time has changed that for
me.

Time, and a sweet brown-eyed boy named James—more on that
soon.

After my family had been worn down by my neurotic puppy lovin'
behavior, they agreed that we should bring home an English mastiff
puppy as our next pet.

I was delighted with their decision, and despite their annoyed
tones and surrendering shrugs, I was certain this was a fantastic idea.
I quickly narrowed down my choice of breeders by the dogs they had
available in color, proximity, and price. I chatted weekly with the one I
chose and bought custom-engraved doggie goodies for our sweet new
boy. Sweet Puppy James, to be exact. You know, because of my favorite

book in the Bible and my obsession with James Taylor. It was the perfect mix. And I was thrilled with myself.

What I didn't know—or more accurately, what I didn't take time
to notice—was that *I* was the only one in our family who was thrilled
about this addition. As the calendar pages turned and my excitement
heightened, I started to pick up on an increased number of eye rolls
when I mentioned James's name. We are an animated family that veers
heavily down the lanes of sarcasm, so the eye rolls alone didn't really
catch me by surprise. However, soon those eye rolls carried accompa-
nying comments such as, "Why do you want such a huge dog, Mom?"
and, "I'm glad you're excited about your new puppy, but it certainly
won't be ours."

My heart twisted. I was pulled between something I really wanted
and had dreamed of, and what the people I loved most wanted. Which,
in reality, shouldn't have even been a close race. But if you haven't
noticed yet, I was at a whole new level of crazy, friend. And reality, or
common sense, wasn't exactly something I picked up on easily.

I wish I had listened when I first felt it. The hesitancy in their voices.
The lack of peace. The frustration from my tribe.

I wish I had put on the brakes before allowing my heart to get more
involved, more set, more in love. And I think that's why I wanted to
share this story with you. To hopefully spare you from the same stum-
bles and heartache that I've endured, no matter what *want* it is you're
currently chasing.

Because, you see, I didn't pay attention to the signs. Instead, I
ignored the whispers and the rolls of the eyes. I continued my conversations with the breeder and let myself believe that all would be well
as soon as they met the sweet little pup. I mean, who can hate a puppy,
right?

We ended up welcoming James into our family a few weeks before
Christmas. He was clumsy, and adorable, and finally mine. I felt as if
I'd waited my whole life for him, but in reality, it had been only a few
years. He was a bit more spirited than most mastiffs, but his big brown

eyes had found their instant place in my heart. His awkward paws were too big for his eight-week frame to handle, and it wasn't long before he tripped...blood showed up in his urine, and we ended up at the emergency vet on a Tuesday evening.

Not five minutes in our home, and we land in puppy ER. Looking back, those moments feel a bit prophetic, and I probably should have taken the hint that this might have been a bad idea. The months that followed seemed to be filled with story after story of unforeseen incompatibility. James hated the car, which led to more than one incident where he pooped all over the backseat, stepped in it, and then jumped over the seats onto our children and me. If you've never tried to drive while holding a 70-pound puppy covered in poop on your lap, I suggest you don't try it. You're definitely not missing out on a fun party.

With every unwanted puppy milestone—like eating a child's toy, peeing all over the floor, and plowing over a wobbly 18-month-old—the Stott tribe became even more frustrated, and I became even more torn.

Previously annoyed eye rolls morphed into full-on yelling spurts by everyone in the house. The baby was knocked over time and time again, and with every puppy antic, the stares I got from my people got sharper. And by this, I mean, in full disclosure, they could cut glass.

Who knew that all it would take to turn an easygoing house of laughter into a ticking time bomb of yelling, crying, and frustration was a pony-sized puppy? The tension in our home was tangible and ever-present, and honestly, everybody was just really, really on edge. Everyone hated James but me, and Logan, our sweet little toddler, was now petrified of him.

As days went on, the words of my friend Bob started echoing through my mind. "Everyone asks, 'How's that working for you?' But the better questions to ask is, 'How's it working for everyone else around you?'" His words caused me to stop in my tracks the first time I heard them a few years back, and I couldn't shake them as I pondered how to navigate this situation. A deep conviction began to fall on my heart about how my selfishness had blinded me from the desires and well-being of my own family.

Over the next few weeks, every puppy-provoked problem sent a ping to my soul. Paul talked about love to the Philippians, and one thing that stuck out to me was this: "Do nothing out of selfish ambition or vain conceit. Rather, in humility, value others above yourselves" (2:3).

Ouch. Somebody pleaaaasssseee let me go back in time and redo this decision. Despite the poopy paws and potty training in the midst of a rainy northwest winter, I had really grown to love this little horse puppy of mine. But the frustration that spilled out of the mouths and eyes of the beloveds I share this life with were casting a huge shadow on my joy.

I began to wonder if it was worth the trouble it was causing.

I spent the next few weeks watching and praying. I didn't want to be hasty, but I also knew the way we were living wasn't working. We had had plenty of animals that worked out just fine after a while. Our first mastiff, which we lost a few years ago, was basically our soul puppy. The whole family loved him. So I knew it wasn't a forever and always issue, or even an English mastiff issue. It was a right now, with this specific dog issue.

Once I finally stopped to pay attention, the answer became glaringly obvious.

As adults, we are responsible for tending to the tone of our home and creating an environment that encourages love, joy, laughter, and peace. If those things aren't present, we need to pay attention and do some atmospheric inventory. Something had shifted drastically in our home that opened us up to a world of walking on eggshells, holding in anger, and no longer being able to connect with each other for fear of hurting someone's feelings with our honesty.

It seems silly that something as small as a dog could make such a big impact, but the truth is, it wasn't James at all. It was that our hearts had become divided. In this season of our lives, we didn't have the margin for such a large commitment. But I was so fixated on James's adorable, droopy eyes, horselike stature, and my desire to fill the void of our first mastiff, that I didn't pause long enough in the planning to even ask the hearts in our own home.

Was this really something they wanted?

Were they really okay with this choice?

Was there another pet that they would have been more excited to welcome into our family?

Was this a case of a good thing at the wrong time?

Did we have margin in our calendar, or finances, or the physical space in our home to get a dog of this size?

Processing those questions in retrospect further illuminated my selfish heart. I was so focused on getting what I wanted that I didn't even stop to consider what the rest of the family wanted. It was a picture-perfect case of surface unity, not soul unity. The whole family had agreed it was okay and said yes to my request. But deep down, this was not what they wanted at all, and my eight- and ten-year-olds were showing more sacrificial love than I was.

Talk about a wake-up call.

My heart became heavy with what my own selfishness had put my family through over the last six months, and I knew it was my turn to change what needed changing. I searched around and found a sweet retired couple who had been on the hunt for a fully trained young mastiff. A few weeks later, Isaac and I drove James out to their family farm in Oregon's wine country and placed his bed near the wood stove in their kitchen.

It felt like a perfect match and a sweet ending to an uncomfortable story.

Even though it was difficult walking away from a pet I'd grown to really care for, seeing peace, calmness, and laughter be restored to our home made it more than worth it.

If love, joy, laughter, and peace aren't PRESENT in your HOME, you need to PAY ATTENTION and do some ATMOSPHERIC INVENTORY.

It's amazing how much tension and stress had been brought into our home because of that decision without my even realizing it. And once James was gone, and everyone seemed to sigh a collective deep breath, it was even more obvious how affected we all were by him.

Looking back, I am so thankful I didn't continue trying to make something work that the people I loved most didn't want to work in the first place.

James has become a lesson to me to explore things further and dig deeper as we make decisions as a family. I can't always take agreement as unity, and maybe you shouldn't either. Especially if you live with amazingly selfless people like I do, or are surrounded by people-pleasing types. Simply agreeing might not be the full story, and it's up to us to explore the hearts that share our home.

We all need to press into the Holy Spirit to help us differentiate between the two, and to help us land at a place that is truly the best way forward.

The more I walk with Jesus, the more I see Him in the little everyday moments, and I'm learning to pay more attention. As I've emptied my calendar and made more room for Him and what matters in my life, I've become more tuned to notice things as they unfold. James's story has shown me that peace is worth fighting for, and that when you can't seem to find it, maybe there's something that needs to be explored, or quite possibly even uprooted.

It's taught me to listen and to wait. And to explore the eye rolls and frustrated tones even if it means I may hear something I don't want to. The people around me are always saying something, even if they aren't talking.

And it's my job, as someone the Lord has placed to steward them, to pay close attention.

23

Trees

*Live in such a way that men may recognize
that you've been with Jesus.*

CHARLES SPURGEON

This morning I woke up to a blanket of white and a sacred silence. The kind of silence that comes after a fresh snowfall that forces the world to be still, to wait. I made my way through the dark, creating creaking footsteps down the hall. The beams of light from our post outside snuck their way through the cracks in the curtains and onto the floor beneath my toes.

I walked, as I always do, straight for the Keurig in the coffee corner beneath Isaac's grandmother's milk glass collection. The sky was navy outside—not black or bright blue, but a hazy navy as it often is this time of morning when the sun has made its way to our neck of the woods but hasn't yet peeked over the mountaintops.

As I poured my creamer and began to stir my coffee, I looked out the window and saw the most beautiful sight along the fence at the edge of our property. Twelve trees, covered in layers of snow, glistening in the sunrise.

The mere sight of them made me gasp and take a second look in disbelief. It was beyond stunning. Something more out of a majestic movie set than my backyard. You may be tilting your head to the side and saying, "Karen, it's just trees and snow. It's not exactly mind blowing." And to that, I'd tell you this: "You're right. It's not mind blowing...Usually."

Snow-covered trees have been the backdrop of my entire upbringing. When you grow up in the Pacific Northwest, you get spoiled by things like towering evergreens dancing under heaven's sugar. So I completely get why this morning's picture would not be shocking.

Yet it was.

I couldn't stop staring at this row of trees at the base of our pasture. I feel it necessary to tell you that the reason I was so enamored with them was because just hours before, as we settled into our evening and I grabbed my bottle of cider looking out the same window, those 12 trees were the bane of my aesthetically obsessed existence.

Every day, for the past, say, 380 days, those trees have tormented me with their sheer ugliness. Now, I love trees with the best of them, but these trees had a personal vendetta to try to eat away at my joy.

Why? Because these trees are dead. All 12 of them. And I mean dead, dead. Every day they taunt me with their brittle, bare brown branches and see-through bodies.

Last year I saved up a lot of money and bought a dozen 11-foot cedar trees to line the fence between us and our neighbor's house down the hill. Our views are my favorite part of this property, and yet the only thing I wanted to change was seeing the side of our neighbor's house, complete with red metal trailers, campers, about seven cars parked at all times, and oodles of garbage cans.

I hope you can hear my dissatisfaction with this situation.

So, shortly after we moved in, I made it my mission to fix the eyesore in the most efficient and beautiful way. We could have built a fence, but somehow that felt weird, being surrounded by farmland. So I set my heart on trees. I called around and found a nursery that carried tall and mature cedars. I made friends with the old man who ran the place, and he suggested red cedars would grow the fastest and provide the most blockage from the neighbors. He referred me to a lawn and garden company who would deliver the trees to me and plant them.

It was the most perfect plan. Until it wasn't.

Shortly after the trees were planted, we got hit with torrential rain and insanely high winds. The trees couldn't handle the impact, and many of them fell over. We put them back in place, staked them, and figured all would be well.

Over the next few months we watched them lose color, and strength, and fullness. Until one day we looked up and were greeted with bare limbs and sparse bunches of orange needles.

I've been meaning to go pull them out for months now, but I couldn't bear to admit the defeat. I'd failed. I couldn't even get trees to grow in the Christmas tree capital of the world. And removing these dead trees from our fence line was like coming to terms with so many of my other failures and heartaches.

So I just left them there. Dead. Barren. A vast display of ugliness and disappointment greeting me and my coffee every morning and causing my soul to grieve with frustration.

Every morning started this way. For nearly 400 mornings.

Until this one.

This morning I looked down upon my tree-lined fence and was met with the magic of heaven. Old made new. Dirty made clean. Ugly putting on the clothes of breathtaking beauty.

I just stood there. Awestruck. I stared harder and harder as I tried to make sense of it, looking with deep intensity trying to see a glimpse of the dead brown limbs under the white, sparkly blanket.

But I couldn't. All I could see was snow. All I could see was this bright, white, shining wall of beauty. Glistening with freshness, and wonder, and a peaceful presence that was almost magical. Okay, let's face it. It was *completely* magical.

My 12 dead trees weren't even recognizable under the glory, and I instantly saw pieces of my own heart wrapped up in their branches. Why do I fight so hard to do everything on my own with a Savior who wants to wash me like snow and cover me in Himself? Why do I insist on believing that I am forgotten? Looked over? And left behind? When I am clearly engulfed by the love of the King?

I bet if those trees could brush away enough snow from their imaginary tree eyes to look in the mirror, they wouldn't even believe what they saw. The beauty on their own bodies. The majesty before them. Completely covering them. Even with the cold of the snow up against their bark and the glory visibly on their frames, they might still feel the sting of ugliness and rejection of not being able to succeed at what they were created to do.

We all do this. Me especially. As I reflect on the last 20 years of my pursuit of God, I can come up with countless times, sadly, when I did this very thing. When I forgot whose I was, and continued to walk down a path clothed in barren not-enough-ness instead of dressing in the fullness that comes with being clothed in Christ.

It feels almost impossible for me to see myself as anything but the small-town high school girl who barely graduated. Somewhere along the line, I started putting on clothes I was never meant to wear. They came in the form of failures, shades of shame, and believing other people's whispers over God's.

And before long, that's how I identified myself.

Even worse, I was convinced that's how everyone else identified me too.

I don't know where you are today, friend. Or where your heart is, for that matter. I don't know if you're flying high or fighting back the tears from yet another broken heart or shattered dream. But I do know that somewhere along the line, we've all believed something about ourselves that we were never meant to believe.

Maybe it's that you will never succeed at what you love like that gal who seems to do so effortlessly.

Maybe it's that you believe you are too old, too young, too single, or too weighed down with mommy duties to pursue anything.

Maybe it's more serious than all of that because someone has wounded your insides and shattered your heart, and you're left trying to sort through the pieces of too many failures, too many upsets, too many tears.

And as you've been trying to learn how to stand up on your own two feet again, you've picked up these lies and used them to help you stand. Never realizing that as long as you still have your hands on them, you'll never stand fully upright.

You've got to let go and stand tall. Forgive that betrayer, and yourself for owning any piece of that tragedy.

Dear one, it's not your fault. So please stop carrying it.

And if in your case it is your fault, give yourself the grace our Savior died for you to have. He didn't die so that we could continue living in our bondage, holding on to our heartache and swallowing lies about ourselves that keep holding us back and shoving us down.

He died so that we could be free. And freedom doesn't wear chains of what was. Freedom lifts off, flies high, and embraces all that He is.

Matthew Henry's commentary says this:

> Being baptized into Christ, we are baptized into his death, that as he died and rose again, so we should die unto sin, and walk in newness and holiness of life. The putting on of Christ according to the Gospel, consists not in outward imitation, but in a new birth, an entire change.

An entire change.

An *entire* change. This entirety forces me to look deep into the eyes of what my heart used to believe. It's causes me to grapple with it. Wrestle it. Make sense of it. It's not a change that encompasses action alone. But the entire being. The soul. The heart. The eyes. The thoughts. The words. The beliefs. Entire. All of it. Without *any* left out.

Putting on the clothes of Christ is a full surrender not to just *walk* in the ways of righteousness but to think through and believe them as well. It's an act of totally surrendering our own look in favor of looking like Him.

We find
what we
have eyes
to see.

Much like the trees that were unrecognizable under the covering of the snow, I want to be unrecognizable under the clothes of Christ. I want to act, and think, and believe in ways that are honoring to the Savior who lives inside me and covers me whole. Where the sins of my past and the yuck of my heart are washed white in snow and shine brightly of the transformation He can do in a life.

I want people to stop in their tracks when they see Him on me. The glistening, blinding sight of dead limbs blanketed in the whitest freshly fallen snow.

Just as I did that morning.

I want unrecognizable newness laced in earth-shattering grace.

Covered whole in Him.

To walk freely in love, and life, and confidence, and service as He intended I would.

And I want that for you too.

24

Fully Here

No one will ever get to the end of their lives and
wish they had spent less time with their children.

ANONYMOUS

Isaac and I make a point to have a blast with our kids. And better yet, we have a blast embarrassing our kids. Not in a rude, hurtful, call-them-out kind of way, but in a let's-chaperone-their-prom-in-'80s-clothes-or-make-out-in-the-kitchen-as-they-cover-their-eyes kind of way.

It's funny that we are like this too because none of our parents were the embarrass-us types. Well, come to think of it, my dad definitely was. So maybe mine came from him. But even still, this laughter-making, laid-back, comfortable love has found its way into our family rhythms and become one of the heartbeats of our home.

And I simply adore it.

It hasn't always been this way, though. For years, more than I care to admit, the atmosphere of our home was more like walking on egg-shells than joining our kids in dance parties and watching them ride laps around our kitchen island on balance bikes.

Isaac is a perfectionist, and I'm a peacemaker. He avoids pain with anger, and I flee uncomfortable conversations in my attempt to avoid all conflict. It's an amazingly brilliant combination. I hope you can sense my sarcasm.

Truth is, it was more like a perfect storm than wedded bliss, and it led to way too many years of fighting, hurting hearts, and shutting down. Until one day, some odd years ago, we just stopped talking about things. The stress and sadness that accompanied these conversations was too much to handle anymore. So we opted out. Denial and avoidance seemed like the only method of survival, and our phones, computers, and laptops became our drugs of choice.

Jumping online and scrolling through the lives of other people took us to a world that allowed us to forget about all of the things weighing down our hearts and minds at home.

Even if for just a moment.

I would get lost in pretty farmhouses adorned with wraparound porches and white furniture with striped pillows, and Isaac zoned out on manly things like tactical guns, camping gear, overland vehicles, and football games.

In those days, our lives were a melting pot of sadness and practicing survival skills from the countless losses, unproductiveness from the overwhelm, and frustration with unmet expectations. Our marriage was rocky because our individual souls were a hot mess, and our work left us drained, unfulfilled, and overwhelmingly exhausted.

It's no wonder we longed for the salve of our screens. Somehow the ache of our own lives hummed a little quieter when we could distract it with the lives of others. And all the while, an addiction was forming and growing stronger with every scroll of our thumbs and double tap of our pointer fingers.

To make matters worse, we were raising tweens. Tweens who were watching us with great intensity and making up laws in their hearts about how the world worked and what their place was in it. I started imagining our house five years down the road, when we had full-on teenagers lounging on our sofas. I imagined the heartache I would feel if I walked into a room filled with gangly bodies and blank stares.

In my imagination I would try to engage and ask a question or bring up a fun conversation, but they wouldn't even look up. I pictured them, tall and possibly awkward, battling their own internal wars, yet sitting at the kitchen table entranced by their screens, disconnected from the very people who could answer questions to help them make sense of their worlds again.

In a brief yet vivid moment of horror, I saw myself. So self-involved, distracted, and completely unaware of the actual life that was unfolding and connecting all around me. How dare I? How dare I give them that as a picture of the world? I couldn't even process what was being uncovered in my own heart, and yet, at the same time, things had never been clearer. This disconnected society we live in was coming after my home with a fierce and alluring vengeance.

It was after my family. After my children. After me.

And I didn't even see it coming.

In Jennie Allen's Bible study *Proven*, a specific phrase in the introduction pierced me straight through the gut. "So if I were your enemy, I would make you numb and distract you from God's story. Technology, social media, Netflix, travel, food and wine, comfort. I would not tempt you with notably bad things, or you would get suspicious. I would distract you with everyday comforts that slowly feed you a different story and make you forget God. Then you would dismiss the Spirit leading you, loving you, and comforting you. Then you would start to love comfort more than surrender, and obedience and souls."

Ouch. Am I the only one who got slapped across the face with conviction from reading these words? Yikes.

Not only was this addiction of mine keeping me from actually enjoying my family and being present, but ultimately, it was distracting me from the only thing that truly matters, God Himself. And His plans for me.

I spent the next several days—okay, months—trying to shift the blame. I made all of the excuses in the book that declared I didn't have to be the first one to change. I mean, let's be real, I own several businesses that require work online, a presence on social media, and answering e-mails. My phone is a very convenient way to cross off a ton of duties while not letting work invade my whole life.

But wait, is it really not invading my whole life?

A less-phone-time concept was beginning to convict my heart. It felt all too familiar, and simultaneously so uncharted. I had to remind myself that only a decade ago I didn't even know what a text message was, and now the majority of my communication was locked up in this tiny three-by-five box I carried in my pocket.

Am I the only one that feels deep sadness about that? Do you?

I felt adult tantrums creeping up and trying to take over my mind, and let's be real, my face too. Isaac always teases me that I am the worst liar on the planet. I guess there are worse things to be bad at, but in the event you actually *want* your face to lie for you, this "my face can't lie" gene is really infuriating.

I wanted to have it all together. I wanted to be the one without the problem. I wanted to be able to sit my family down, have a *Brady Bunch*–style family meeting, and declare to them that we had a new rule about gadgets and there were about to be some *big* changes around our home. The problem, though, was that this epiphany of mine had nothing to do with tightening the reins on these tiny humans I was raising, and everything to do with tightening *my* reins.

As much as I don't want to admit it, what my kids are learning about how the world works and what they take on as their own habits starts with me. I can't sit them down and lecture them on excessive iPad habits if I myself am so engrossed in scrolling, or work, or responding to one last e-mail that I don't even realize they are speaking to me.

I can't give them 20-minute time limits if I don't honor the same rules, and worse, work on the computer all night while completely ignoring the hearts in my own home.

"Just a minute, honey" was a phrase I spoke way too often. And let's be real, it was never just one more minute. That minute usually lasted for hours, sometimes days, and I needed to make it stop.

It feels so surfacey and unmeaningful to talk about gadgets and gizmos aplenty. Yet here I sit, typing away on the very thing that has the power to take over my entire life—and my heart too—if I'm not careful.

As insignificant as it can seem to bare my techy addictions and admit to being a productivity-driven workaholic, I feel not mentioning these things would be far more damaging. This behavior of mine held the power to significantly change the course of my home and my history. So I feel I owe it to you, and to myself, to at least broach the subject.

It's a problem that my three-year-old brings me my phone from the kitchen because he's been trained to always see me with it. It's a problem when Isaac has to get my attention because one of our kids is trying to tell me something and I don't even notice they are talking. It's a problem that we as a society tend to text a family member from the other room of the same house instead of just getting up, walking over to them, and engaging in a real conversation. It's a problem going on a date, or a trip, or being in a conversation and I just can't stop touching my phone!

Often Isaac asks me what I am doing, or what I am looking at, and I don't even have an answer. Truth is, I don't even know what I was looking at. I just started pressing buttons, swiping, and scrolling without having the slightest idea why. Or equally as bad, I may be checking my phone for a valid reason, but I haven't mastered the self-control to wait five minutes till the kids are in bed to do so.

What in the actual world was wrong with me? I wish I was an isolated case, the only one with this issue, but I have a sense that very few of us are immune to this techy epidemic.

To be quite honest, it hurts my heart when I go to someone's house for dinner and they play games on their tablet or phone instead of engaging with me. Or worse, when they *think* they are engaging with me, but it's more like nodding and murmuring, "Yeah...uh-huh...yeah...okay..." and they don't take their eyes off the screen. This was a huge wake-up call to help me beat my own habits of doing the same thing to the kids.

It hurts when I walk into a room full of people who are together, but not really. It hurts when I see couples at dinner laughing about something they are reading on their phones instead of causing their loved one right in front of them to laugh.

This isn't normal, friend. And it's not healthy.

Somehow our society has morphed into a world where disconnect and *Truman Show*–type broadcasting of our lives has trumped actually being present in our real ones.

What hurts the most is knowing that I have been more of a participant than a spectator in almost every area I listed above. I hate to think that I may have caused, or may still cause, any member of my family or the people I share my actual life with to feel less than or not worthy of my time because I couldn't wait until I was alone to check my phone.

And for what? So I can see what game someone else is playing with their kid instead of playing one with mine? It's crazy, right?

All of this gadgety talk is starting to make me feel a little crazy. I wish with every part of my being that this wasn't an issue. I wish that we as a society hadn't gone here in the first place. That *I* hadn't.

But we have. And I love my family and you, dear reader, too much to ignore it any longer.

I am a serious phone-loving, e-mail-checking, text-sending workaholic mama who gets way too pumped up on productivity. And I really have a problem.

Well, *had* a problem. They say that the first step is admission, right? And it definitely was for me. Still is on occasion, if I don't keep myself in check. But being honest about it was the first and hardest step. Once I identified the problem, it somehow lost a bit of its power. I was aware, so I was accountable. It weakened after it came to the surface, which was mind blowing to me. And seemingly in an instant, it went from a problem to a process.

I want to live a LIFE where the PEOPLE I LOVE and those I'm AROUND know they matter. And even more than that, I want them to know that they are SEEN and they are WORTH IT. WORTH my TIME. WORTH my EYE CONTACT. WORTH being HEARD.

And for me, a huge part of it was allowing my loved ones into my mess, and giving them the freedom to call me out and keep me accountable when they saw me breaking one of my own rules.

Now I have more of an ongoing journey than a huge problem. I get to choose daily which path I will take, what I will pick up, and what I will put down.

It all started with a choice. And now I get to keep choosing every day, sometimes by the minute, what is going to win my time. My family, or my phone. But I had to engage the battle as a battle. I couldn't keep ignoring the issue or wait for others in my house to change first. It would have been easy for me to feel I had to change only when my kids changed or when my husband changed. But that's not very adult now, is it?

I had to be the one to embrace a new rhythm and chart a new path, no matter what anyone else in my house chose to do. I had to set new boundaries and make the tough calls for myself and pray they'd follow.

Someone always has to be the first to apologize. The first to jump. The first to dare to live differently. And as much as I wish it didn't have to be me, why shouldn't it be? Why should I wait for someone else to take control of their life and live with no regrets before I do?

I don't really know how we as a culture got this far off the path so quickly, but it's actually a bit frightening. When our oldest was in kindergarten, I still had a flip phone. I didn't even know how to send a text message, or what that even was.

But in the past eight years, we've gotten uncomfortably off course, and it's my responsibility to make sure that, for me and my home, we find our way back to a healthy balance. The digital world is a fascinating place, and a huge blessing if we use it right. But just like my favorite chocolate peanut butter swirl brownies, too much, left unchecked, is going to make you sick.

And it's just not worth it.

I want to live a life of being fully available and fully present for the ones I love. And for too long I've lived a life so maxed out with my own little world, responsibilities, and career aspirations that I haven't had room in my mind or margin in my heart for the loves of my life that I share my actual days with.

My striving for professional success left no room for my husband, my kids, my extended family, and my friends. And that's simply not the legacy I wanted to leave.

Jesus modeled love with His availability, and I'd hate to think that I could miss out on the life He has for me, or worse, teach my kids to tune out what He has for them, because I am too distracted, over-scheduled, or simply too invested in the online world to be fully alive in my real one.

I want to live a life where the people I love and those I'm around know they matter. And even more than that, I want them to know that they are seen and they are worth it.

Worth my time. Worth my eye contact. Worth being heard.

I want to sit down for coffee, or lunch, or dinner, and have them all know that I am with them, Fully. No distractions. With so much of the world vying for my attention, it's an ongoing battle, sweet friend. A fierce one. This digital age and the world of social media are alluring. But I can't think of a battle more worthy of engaging in than the one that's trying to distract me from time with God, with my kids, and living my own life.

As a business owner, it wasn't realistic for me to say that I was going to just stop being on my phone. But it was realistic for me to say that I'm going to set up boundaries so that my kids rarely see me on my phone. I'm not saying I do this 100 percent of the time because that wouldn't be realistic either, but keeping this ideal at the forefront of my mind has really helped me conquer the struggle.

Instead of carrying my phone around with me all the time now, I keep it in another room while I'm at home. If I need to post something to my business social media accounts or check my e-mail, I go to the garage for a few minutes and take care of those tasks between switching the laundry. Then, when the task is complete, I bring the phone back in the house, usually on top of a basket of peppermint-scented laundry, and I put it back in my room.

Out of sight, out of mind, and most importantly, out of my hands!

If I were to go somewhere comfortable, like my bed or the office, to check in on things or make a post, I'd be tempted to get sucked in longer and knock more things off of my to-do list. But the garage is ideal. There's nowhere to sit, and it's not exactly cozy. It's the perfect place to sneak away to and get something done quickly without getting lost in it. And it's working brilliantly.

I've also asked my kids to keep me accountable, which was an incredibly hard decision, but one I don't regret in the slightest. Our kids know now that their voices matter. That they matter. They know that their opinions mean something and carry enough weight to actually make changes. And *that* is huge. And it's been fun for me too. They love keeping me in check, and I love the reminders. Because they nudge me closer to the person and the mama I want to be.

I know these changes are a little extreme, and they may not work in everyone's situation, but if you're serious about doing things differently, it's definitely worth the work of finding something that does. I was extremely ready to take back my life and be more in tune with those I love the most. So for us, it's been a welcome change.

I can't even explain the joy I found when I decided to put that beast down and look into eyes instead of screens. I'm listening more, stressed less, and I find myself even laughing again, which I'm sad to say I didn't even realize I was missing until I found it.

I feel awake, and alive, and deeply connected to myself, my people, and my world again.

And the new view is breathtaking.

25

Nooks and Notes

Any building is a temple. If you make it so.

PHIL KNIGHT

For as long as I can remember I've been a home person. An aesthetics person. I've always cared about design, and details, and decorating my walls in the most beautiful ways. I can still remember designing my childhood bedroom with pink walls, white kitten stencils, and the loveliest vintage shabby-chic rose-pattern bedding. It was pure eight-year-old bliss, and I adored every inch of it.

As I made my way into my teenage years, I did everything I could to turn my ten-by-ten little room into an actual tiny house—before those were even a thing. My room was complete with a futon, a small round dining table that I used as a desk, and a full-size piano. How, I'm not quite sure, but we made it work, and I loved it. Something in me just longed for my own little space. My own little home, even back then.

It was my personal temple. My sacred space.

Growing up I felt like the odd duck in so many ways. I was the teenage girl who'd rather peruse the aisles of Lowe's or Home Goods than the racks at Nordstrom or Forever 21. I wanted to stay home and repaint garage sale furniture or make my own pillows instead of going to the movies with my friends. I don't think anything has ever been more exciting for me, as long as I can remember, than cultivating a safe, secure, and over-the-top beautiful space.

Now, as an adult, I've carried this love affair into all nine homes Isaac and I have shared together. From one-bedroom apartments and double-wide trailers to the custom home we had built and our military housing overlooking the Gulf of Mexico. Each one of them has been a passion project of reinventing a space and taking it from something ordinary to something truly magical.

Even if it's just magical for me and my people.

Having beautiful spaces filled with meaningful treasures deeply matters to me. And I've always wondered where this came from. After my grandpa passed away, I became even more obsessed with our Danish heritage. I've always been very interested in it, and have found ways to incorporate my Scandinavian roots into our rhythms, but something changed after he died. And all I wanted to do was find out more about this wonderland he came from.

I guess I thought that learning more about the culture and the way people did life there might give me more glimpses into how he became the incredible man he was.

And maybe, just maybe, how I became who I am too.

Turns out, this aesthetically inclined way of living is, in fact, very Danish. Which kind of blew my mind. In Helen Russell's book *The Year of Living Danishly*,* she spends a year researching the country to try to uncover their secrets of being the world's happiest country. During her time living there, she discovered that "Denmark is very much a design society, and that plays quite a big part in happiness...In 2011, scientists at University College London studied this phenomenon and confirmed that looking at something beautiful really can make us happier by stimulating dopamine in our brains...Research shows that great art and design can even induce the same brain activity as being in love."

Being intentional with the aesthetic of your environment is just the way of life for Danes. In an interview with the author, a Danish woman said, "We are simply used to having nice surroundings. It starts from the very beginning of life. Children come to school and interact

---

* Helen Russell, *The Year of Living Danishly* (London: Icon Books, 2015).

with quality architecture and furniture, and so from an early age they develop an understanding that functional yet beautiful design is essential to realizing the good life...And of course, the weather plays a part too. We're inside so much during the long winters that we invest more in our environment. You're spending so much time at home, it may as well be nice!...There is a clear relationship between your aesthetic environment and how you feel."

Amen, my Danish sister. As I read these words, I felt my insides leap out of my chest into a standing ovation. And I became even giddier that my antique-hoarding, dish-obsessed, dinner-party-decorating self now had research to back up the benefits of such time investments.

As our climate here in Oregon greatly mimics that of my Scandinavian homeland, a lightbulb went off when I read these words, and I became even more committed to creating a beautiful, inviting, inspirational, and cozy home.

"You're spending so much time at home, it may as well be nice!"

My sentiments exactly.

It's surprising that I am even dressed most days in something more than my husband's T-shirts, as spending money on clothing makes me want to roll my eyes and crawl into a hole. Unless your name is Lulu Lemon and your clothing doubles as sleepwear and workout attire, or leggings I can transform into date-night wear with a pretty sweater, you're dead to me.

But pillows. And throws. And milk glass everything, and succulents in handmade monochrome pots.

Take. All. My. Money.

I may sound like a loon, and that's okay too. But I think there is something so intricately important about the environments we place ourselves in and invite others into.

There's magic in the way a light-filled room can restore a soul, and a cozy chair with an intentionally chosen stack of books and magazines holds the power to ignite dreams, bring rest, and inspire creativity.

A well-designed place gives our souls space to breathe and our minds a welcomed rest. It becomes the backdrop for dinners and dance parties, and a safe place to land when something wrecks our world and we don't know which way is up.

If we desire it to be, our home can be more than just a landing pad for our weary bodies to find food and hang our clothes. Our homes hold the power to be absolutely transformative.

They hold the power to hold us and tend to us. To shelter people and offer grace. To heal wounds and take the first step to mend that broken relationship. They can be a blank space to dream dreams and a refuge when you need to recharge.

I don't believe we were created to be go, go, go people all the time. God isn't up in heaven right now preparing an obstacle course or a checklist for us when we see Him face-to-face.

He's up there, right now, preparing for us a home. A table. A seat.

About a month ago, my last remaining grandparent passed away an hour or so after I held her hand, kissed her hot, fevered forehead, and prayed Jesus would take her home as my tears fell silently to the cold tile floor.

It had been about ten months since my grandpa, her husband of 67 years, had left us here on earth to see his home in heaven. And although my heart broke watching her go, there was a sweet peace knowing they were finally together again. Ten months apart really must have been agony after a lifetime together.

In the weeks that followed her death, my mother and I cleaned out her and Grandpa's apartment and sorted through things. It was a lot like the process of moving, but sadder. What gets thrown away, given away, donated? What do we keep?

Two lives gone. The accumulation of their lives and their histories in a one-bedroom apartment. We went through boxes and drawers, sifting through staplers, extra stamps, and bookshelf after bookshelf of their favorite stories and photo albums. We paused to show each other what we had found and reminisce about some of the best souls each of us had ever known.

My grandparents were huge history buffs, and I'm certain my grandma was the first person ever to sign up for an account on ancestry. com. Or maybe the first person over the age of 60, but we'll never know for sure. They loved keeping their heritage alive and placed immense importance on family heirlooms, history, and family trees.

Dozens, if not hundreds, of times we'd pull something out of a nook or a box, turn it over, and find a tiny sticker with my grandmother's handwriting on the bottom.

- Crocheted tablecloth: "By Nora (Carl's aunt) in Denmark."
- Candelabra: "From Copenhagen. A friend gave this to Jorgen and Anna (my great-grandparents) in 1955. It is typical of candleholders in Danish churches, and always had a prominent, visible place in the home."
- Pump organ: "Purchased off a traveling wagon in Franklin, Oregon, in 1895."
- Pine chest: "Handmade by Jorgen in his kitchen. He made one for his wife and 7 of his children."
- Rolling pins: "From Anna and Zella."

Before these moments going through what she had left behind with my mother, before I couldn't hug her anymore or bake zucchini bread in her kitchen anymore, I hadn't understood why she held on to these things. Or wrote about them with such great detail.

But I understand now.

Grandma wanted to hold on to the memories as long as she could. She wanted the history of her loved ones to stay alive and their stories to be passed down.

She wanted them to matter to the future generations as much as they'd mattered to her.

And I get it now.

Because I feel the same way about keeping her and Grandpa's memories alive.

Growing up in a home that carried on many of these traditions, I've always thought that this was normal. Everyone has a house full of hand-me-down treasures from their great-great-great-grandparents, right?

But apparently it's not something everyone does. Or has. And I'm increasingly thankful that it's something my family fought to keep alive.

I'm thankful that my legacy isn't just in stories but in stuff as well. Stuff that I could never find in the aisles of my beloved Target.

For some reason, that seems clearer now after the last year. I've always collected home things from the people I love. And looking back, I'm even more thankful for it now as I've seen firsthand what it looks like to sort through what's left behind.

I've found myself lately reflecting on what that will look like for my children one day. I don't want to have a house full of all of the latest and greatest styles and mass-produced everything. If I'm going to choose what I fill my house with, which I get to do, I want to choose with purpose. I want to fill the space between our walls with books that mean something, decorations that hold stories, and vases that held my grandmother's flowers.

There's a peace that comes with outfitting my house in this way. It's instantly home, no matter what actual house we are in. Because those same items have been making my family's houses into homes for generations.

I love that my children get to play piano on the same keys my grandpa used to fill his house with music.

That they get to read from his Bible, all worn from carrying in his pocket every day he served during World War II.

I love that our pitchers, and creamers, and some of our favorite coffee mugs were held by the hands of other generations before they ever touched mine.

I want to fill the SPACE between our walls with BOOKS that mean SOMETHING, decorations that HOLD STORIES, and VASES that held my GRANDMOTHER'S flowers.

That the same hand-crocheted doilies adorned their Thanksgiving tables before we even existed. And now the great-great-grandchildren of those who stitched them together are carefully setting the table with them. And rolling out piecrusts with the same wooden rolling pins they used in their kitchens.

What an unbelievable gift I've been given that I didn't even know I wanted.

I'm evermore tired of having stuff for stuff's sake, and all the more into holding things that hold stories. It takes work, and intention, and lots of creativity to incorporate some of these things into our style sometimes, but I'm committed to doing everything I can to keep making it work.

And hopefully, if I play it right, my great-great-grandchildren will want to make it work too.

I want to add that if you're reading this and have a similar story, my heart leaps with thankfulness for you. But I also know that this is rare, and that having a history of housewares isn't something that everyone has. Friend, I'm so sorry about that. But here's the good news. We get to change our legacy.

In the same way that we can change a family history of divorces, or debt, or anger to legacies of staying, and being free, and living full of joy, we have the power and the choice to change this legacy too.

We can start telling stories. We can start writing notes and keeping things we find special.

Isaac and I have placed notes in the glass we used for communion at our wedding. We've kept things from our children's baby years and every one of Isaac's fire helmets from his years of service.

We keep our children's baby clothes to make quilts out of, and gifts we've given each other over the years. I have a giant plastic tub that contains every card, note, Post-it, and letter Isaac and I have written to each other over the last 18 years.

And I have one for the kids' notes too.

Even though it's not very nostalgic, we love getting our Instagram feeds printed into tiny eight-by-eight books that we keep on our dresser, and I'm constantly finding them laid out all over our bed as the kids laugh and reminisce over the memories. They aren't fancy, and they aren't as pretty as my grandma's handwritten leather journals, but they're ours, and I wouldn't trade them for the world.

Because in all of these little things we hold on to, what makes them so magical is that it's us. It's our family. Our heritage. Our story.

And it's one worth telling, and retelling.

No matter what we've been given by our family, we can choose to keep our family's story alive through heirlooms too. We can start today. With that necklace you love, or that scarf you knit, or that photo you took.

They all hold stories, if we just choose to tell them.

26

Roots

*What screws us up the most in life is the picture
in our head of what it's supposed to be.*

ANONYMOUS

Most of my life I've had this bitter angst about the mountains. I don't know what it is, but sometimes when hurt enters our stories, the backdrop can take the blame. What used to be simple geography can take on a life of its own, bringing back painful memories and almost taunting us with smells, visuals, and other triggers.

The forests of the Pacific Northwest used to hold that pain for me. The trees, the wet ground, the soggy, earthy smell of it all. It was almost like they were speaking to me. Taunting me. "You can't do this. You will never, ever amount to anything. So why even try?"

For years it was almost like this place would whisper to my thoughts. Plaguing me with an echoing voice, "You're worthless. Nothing. You'll never make it." And somehow, the gray Oregon skies and dripping wet forests I grew up in seemed to reinforce those thought patterns.

Sometimes I would wish I could fly somewhere else that looked more promising. Over the years I'd found it was simpler to run away from pain instead of staying and having to stand and face the giants in my own home.

During these years as I processed the pain and wanted to run, I became consumed with all things *Southern Living*. I dreamed of rolling hills, large front porches, and kids with cute accents. I planned where we would go on vacation if we lived there, where we would probably go to church, and who we would do life with if we moved.

Remember James? And my propensity to go all-in before I've walked through the proper check systems? Yeah, well...welcome to James 1,000 times over.

I became obsessed with moving, and my drive to get where I wanted further deepened my frustration for where I actually was. It no longer mattered to me that Isaac loved the mountains and the snow, and that our kids did too. It didn't make a difference to me that all of our family lived here, and moving would rip us out of everyday relationships with grandparents, cousins, and lifelong family friends.

Selfish much? I know...it was bad. And I shudder when I think back on one of the worst versions of myself.

I could no longer see the good things about staying in Oregon, and my joy was suffocating because of it. My eyes had become focused on myself alone, and all I could see was what I wanted. Somehow the man I loved more than life became the wall that was standing between me and my dreams

What on earth? How does that even happen?

But that's what deception does. Deception turns our eyes inward so all we can see is our own point of view. Even if it's not the truth. Sometimes we can get so focused on the things that we think will make us happy, and what we want for our own life, that our dreams actually become our gods. And our true God, and the plans that He has for our lives, drown in the wake of our own goals and plans.

This is where I was, friend. And it was dangerous territory. Sadly, as I watch the world around me, I get the sense that much of society is in this same place. I've watched wives walk away from husbands, mothers walk away from children, people step away from their calling, and even Christians turn their back on biblical truths, all in the name of "It just doesn't feel right anymore." Or, "It's just not what I want for my life anymore. We want different things. This can't possibly work anymore."

Every time I hear a story like this, my heart breaks a little bit more.

And the worst part...it was almost my story too.

I almost let deception win and my own selfishness lead me down a very dangerous path.

I almost lost everything.

And I couldn't be more thankful that God, in His great grace, woke me up and snapped me out of it.

I've learned so much in the past several years, as God, in His gentlemanly ways, guided me through. And to my complete surprise, helped me love the mountains and the forests again too. But, friend, something came out of this experience that shook me all the way through.

> We weren't put on this earth to fulfill our great dream. We were put on this earth to follow God's great plan.

We weren't put on this earth to make us feel good. We aren't called into marriage to make sure all of our own needs are met, or placed into a career or calling to fill ourselves up with happy thoughts and alluring accolades. We weren't even put here to make sure we feel completely fulfilled in the work we do every day or in the homes we run.

And I know writing this is not making me the most popular gal in your eyes right now either. But I think this is a big thing that as a society we've gotten mixed up lately. We weren't put on this earth to fulfill our great dream. We were put on this earth to follow God's great plan. And oftentimes, sticking it out, staying put, and swapping our dream for His are the prerequisites to seeing this beautiful plan unfold.

We need to allow our circumstances to refine us, to make us better people. We are called to be a reflection of Him, not a resemblance of society. We were placed where we are, in the families, the marriages, the cities, the schools, the jobs, and the locations we find ourselves in, to stand out for His name.

That's what this whole thing of life is about in a nutshell.

Mirroring His character.

Echoing His words.

Declaring His greatness.

Telling His story through our testimonies.

When the world says that the loving thing to do in your marriage is to be okay with drifting apart, or to walk away if you aren't happy anymore, it is lying.

When the world says, "Hold that grudge. Make them change before you give in," it is lying.

When the world says, "If it feels good, do it" or "Everything you want is on the other side of fear," it is lying.

These messages simply are not true. At least if you are filtering things through the Word of God, they're not. I would love for my grandparents to still be here, and for our cars not to break down, or not to have lost our house and life savings when the economy crashed. I would love for those things not to be our reality. But fear has nothing to do with any of those things. Getting to the other side of fear won't bring my grandparents back or magically make our cars run or reverse the housing crash.

> Everything you want is on the other side of faith.

So can we all please just stop saying that?

I think a more appropriate quote for believers would be, "Everything you want is on the other side of faith." Faith means I will get to see my grandparents again on the other side, and that I can trust that even though our house and our finances don't currently look like we planned they would, God has good *in* it. He is faithful. And He will complete a good work because that is what His Word promises He will do.

We need to stop taking things at the words of the world and start taking things at God's Word. The Bible is full of stories of men and women who were called to do things that didn't feel good but greatly reflected the love, faithfulness, and character of God. And that's how we need to be looking at our lives, and our marriages, and our friendships, and even our jobs at times.

I'm sure it didn't feel good when Mary and Joseph traveled through the night, pregnant and alone, to give birth in a stable, or when Joseph's brothers sold him into slavery, or when our perfect Jesus spread His arms wide in surrender to the lashings, and mockers, and nails.

Following God doesn't always feel good, but it does feel right.

I'll never forget the day my understanding of faith and feelings changed. During one of my times with the Lord, He whispered to my heart, "What if things never changed? What if your home situation and finances remained like this forever? Would you be okay?"

After mulling it over, I realized that if I knew now that things were never, ever going to change, I would be living a whole lot differently.

I wouldn't be as focused on moving, or what was next, or what life could be like if I got everything I wanted. I would be living like today was the very best gift, and maybe I'd learn to laugh again too.

If I knew that this was it for me, I would be sowing into our city more, and volunteering at our schools, and getting to know the families of our kids' friends. I would work on healing instead of running. I would stop blaming the state, and the trees, and my husband for things that aren't their fault. And I'd open my eyes to the incredible beauty and freedom and adventure that staying holds.

I would be cultivating everything that we currently have and trying to get it to grow instead of demanding a different seed, or a different garden, or a different life.

I would simply live. And be thankful for living. And I'd wake up every day and do the very best I could with what I have right here.

We miss so much when we can't take our mind off of what could be.

A lightbulb went off in my mind that day, and conviction washed over me with a cleansing newness like the washing of Oregon's legendary rains. One of my actual favorite things about this place. As much as I pretend to hate my roots, I'm starting to think they might just be the very best parts of me. Because they keep me humble and true. This is where I found my fight and learned to dig my feet into the ground for things that burdened my heart.

God found me in these parts. He met me in these trees.

In the broken, crumbly bits of darkness where I tried to run, He found me. And He picked me up. And He's been putting me back together and bringing hope through my hurts ever since.

I started to realize that it's not as much about my painful story as it is about His powerful sacrifice. Everything I've endured vanishes in the light of what He endured for me. What He endured for all of us.

I know what it's like to feel the burn of betrayal and the emptiness of abandonment. Those are real things. In my life, and maybe in yours too. And I don't want to make light of them, or tell you to tuck them away too soon or to get over them prematurely. There's definitely a place for them, and they need space and time and tending for you to become whole again.

But I'm learning that reflecting Jesus is more about sharing the liberation of His life than continuing to circle around the hard pieces of mine. I need to keep my eyes focused on the freedom I'm living today, not the failures of my yesterdays.

And maybe that's encouragement for you too.

Now that I've found my way out of the woods, I need to stop turning around and bringing all of the crud of the past into the new seasons with me. At some point, I need to move out of my bondage in order to help others find their way out too. I can't help anyone find their way into freedom if I keep circling around and picking up my own chains.

And isn't that the point? To use our story to help heal others? To move on, to embrace freedom, to keep living this full and beautiful life whole and overflowing with all of the good things so we can lead people to Him? Teach them to keep walking? Help them to keep fighting? Encourage them to keep loving?

Just as He's done in our stories?

Isn't that the whole point?

As I began to open up my eyes to the life God had blessed me with instead of focusing on the life I thought I wanted and didn't have, I began to see Him everywhere. It's not about where I live or where I don't. And it's certainly not about placing the blame on trees and mountains when they obviously aren't responsible. It's not about my job, or ministry, or marriage, or kids, or hobbies. It's about what *He* has done in those things, and getting the honor of reflecting His goodness to others through it.

I see Him in the sunrises over the hills surrounding my house and in the pink buds on the trees in the orchard out front. I see Him in the farmers' markets and in the family I'm surrounded with, and I'm filling up with deep appreciation for where I have been placed.

It just took letting go.

Letting go of the map I had made for my life and embracing His. And as I've let Him invade my heart in this area, I've found that He's invaded my eyes too. He's enabled me to see all the goodness that was waiting right in front of me this whole time. Just beckoning me to open my eyes and find it.

> As I began to open up my eyes to the life God had blessed me with instead of focusing on the life I thought I wanted and didn't have, I began to see Him everywhere.

I'm Grateful For...

27

Rhythms

Traditions are the guideposts driven deep in our subconscious minds. The most powerful ones are those we can't even describe, aren't even aware of.

ELLEN GOODMAN

We all count down the days like children. Eager and excited for what's about to unfold. Giddy with anticipation. We start planning months in advance, and everyone knows what's coming. There is definitely a place for spontaneity and adventure. I'm a firm believer in them both. But what lights my heart on fire more than packing the kids' suitcases and surprising them with Disneyland the day after Christmas are the sacred rhythms that become as much a part of us as our very breath.

Our traditions.

Isaac and I were the first kids on either side of our family to get married. We were the first ones to make any of our parents grandparents. We were the line in the sand. The mold-breakers from one generation to the next. As our siblings continued to go home for Christmas, expecting the same traditions that they grew up with, we weren't exactly sure where we fit in as a newly married and very young couple.

I remember early on when my mom came to me and said, "You two are your own family now. You need to hold that close. Protect it. Decide now what is important to you and what you want to do with your children when you have them so everyone knows what to expect. If you start doing what everyone else wants you to now, they will always expect it. Choose your traditions now and guard them."

> It was the little, seemingly insignificant things we intentionally did, year after year, celebration after celebration, that wove the fabric of our family memories.

Her words exploded through me like fireworks, and something inside me was ignited. I've always been a traditions and celebrations gal. Feasts, and tablescapes, and houses full of people make me come fully alive. But there was something so exhilarating about carving my own path and paving the way for my own family that lit me up inside on a whole new level. Her words freed me, and I knew I had been given a precious gift that I needed to cultivate well.

From that day on, Isaac and I began mapping out all of the holidays and forming our ideas of how we wanted to celebrate them and what we wanted the culture of our family to look like. I knew from my own childhood that it wasn't necessarily the things that cost the most money that marked the pages of my mind. It was the little, seemingly insignificant things we intentionally did, year after year, celebration after celebration, that wove the fabric of our family memories.

Over the last 16 years, our most beloved rhythms have come in the form of waking up to balloon-covered floors and favorite sugar cereals at the breakfast table every birthday morning. It's been Starbucks hot chocolate and snowman cookies before we drove around to look at Christmas lights, and aebleskivers for breakfast (a Danish tradition I grew up with) every Christmas morning.

We find our way back to the same vacation spot in central Oregon every summer and make trips to the family lake cabin built by my dad and grandfather a priority. We plant gardens and get apple cider donuts on our trips to the pumpkin patch, and Isaac and Ava go to the father-daughter dances.

Traditions *are the* BUILDING BLOCKS *of our* family LEGACIES.

We wanted the little things in our lives to end up being the big things. And I think we've made good on that dream.

When the kids were young and I started to dream about their childhoods, I remember looking at it in reverse. Instead of picturing them as toddlers and kindergartners, I imagined them as young married adults, college kids, and high schoolers. I remember asking myself what would be important to them when they looked back on their upbringing and intentionally worked backward from there. I remember specifically trying to think about traditions that would mean a lot to them when they were little, but that they would still want to take part in when they were 16, and 26, and 46.

We decided early on that it would be fun to go on overnight girlie dates and man adventures with the kids each year before school started. Being someone who's a bit high maintenance married to someone who loves camping and the outdoors, this felt like a perfect fit. Ava and I get to go to a fancy hotel and order room service while we watch girlie movies and do our nails. The boys, on the other hand, get their fill of campfires, mountain biking, burping, and getting dirty as they set out to the mountains for their time together every fall.

It may seem silly, or even extravagant, to spend this much money for intentional time with our kids. But one of the things that has always stuck with me is this idea that we, their parents, are in charge of their childhood memories. We get the responsibility and the honor of crafting the foundation of their next 60 years after they leave our home. We are writing the book of their growing-up years, and I want the story of their childhoods to be an anthem of simple, everyday savorings mixed in with grand gestures of extraordinary love.

God modeled this same thing by sending Jesus to live on earth as a man, serving and loving His small community day in and day out while also allowing room for water-to-wine miracles and raising people from the dead.

Loving well isn't all mundane, or all miracles. It's a beautiful dance that intertwines the two and creatively shows off various aspects of God's character as we walk it out.

I think the most important thing about traditions is made up in the memories of them. Which ones are going to stick? Which ones can you do in any season, in any financial situation, in any location? What is going to say the most that you are loved? Thought of? Seen?

> Loving well isn't all mundane, or all miracles. It's a beautiful dance that intertwines the two and creatively shows off various aspects of God's character as we walk it out.

When I look back on growing up, there is so much I gloss over or have forgotten about. But summers at the family lake and aebleskivers on Christmas morning are among the first things that bring a smile to my face.

As my children have grown older and can now look me straight in the eyes, it's become more and more real that our time with them is fleeting fast. I want their childhood to stick. I want them to look back on the time we all spent together as a family within the same walls and have it bring tears and smiles to their faces for the rest of their lives.

I also want the time we have together to set an expectation for how they should be treated by others. If we love them well, give them the freedom to be fully themselves, accept them for who they are, and spoil them anyway, they'll grow to expect the same love and honor from others, and eventually, that will be what they look for in a spouse. And hopefully, prayerfully, they won't settle for anything less.

The world is after our children's hearts with a vengeance. All of its songs and movies and seducing storylines are showing our kids a twisted view of love and dating and acceptance. As their parents, it is our honor and duty to love our kids so well, so extravagantly, and so safely that they won't be tempted to bite on the counterfeit love the world offers.

And I guess that's where my passion for tradition stems. It's the routines that my children remember that remind them of how special they are. It's the rhythms we share together that weave the tapestry of their childhood and may even help them pave the way for their own family rituals one day. I want to take every opportunity I can to shower them with love, attention, intentional conversations, and fun adventures because the memories of their childhood are worth it.

> It is our honor and duty to love our kids so well, so extravagantly, and so safely that they won't be tempted to bite on the counterfeit love the world offers.

This is why we have a fancy breakfast for dinner on Valentine's Day and help them grow their own gardens in the spring. It's why we sometimes play hooky from school to watch the newest movie on their list and why we never pass up a photo booth.

When I stop to think about it, traditions are really the building blocks of our family legacies. They make up what we are remembered for and what is talked about when we are no longer here. It all comes startlingly into focus when I look at it as the way our family will be remembered when I'm no longer here to cultivate it.

What do I want that to look like?

What do you?

What experiences and memories do you want your children to share with their spouses or your grandkids someday?

What do you hope your children will pick up and pass on to their families?

For me it's movie nights and candlelight dinners. It's funny photo booth pictures plastering our fridge and exploring the fields around our house in search of ladybugs...and berries, and frogs. It's balloons and birthday cereal, bonfires with Dad, dance parties in the living room, and Isaac and I holding each other close as we dance in the kitchen.

I want to be remembered for being accepting of who each of my children uniquely is, and for being a springboard that helps launch them each in their own way. I want to be a home of celebration, and adoration, and feeding all the people my people bring home.

I want them to remember throwing kind words and forgiveness around as often as we do Nerf bullets. And have them look back and smile about our picnics in the living room and finding love notes around the house. I want them to laugh about our baking competitions and riding scooters around the kitchen island after dinner.

I want their memories to overflow with play, and possibility, and a sense of deep peace. Where they know they always have a safe place to land, a family who'll always listen, and there will always be aebleskivers on Christmas morning.

Have It All

*Contentment is essentially a matter of accepting
from God's hand what He sends because we know
that He is good and therefore it is good.*

LINDA DILLOW

There are times in life where I stop long enough to soak it all in. Where the hustle fades and the laughter rises. Where I can sit on our patio and watch the horses graze and the sun fall. It's in those times where I can almost feel the tangibleness of God.

He seems close, and touchable, and moving in everything.

And at the risk of sounding completely granola, it's almost as if His creation itself is speaking to me. Those moments, though rarer than I would like, remind me what it's like to feel alive again, and they act as a marker in my heart that we actually survived the heartache that unfolded over the last seven years.

Sadly, these euphoric, "God is so amazing, and all of this pain is so worth it" times aren't exactly my go-to response. I tend to be a bit of a hot mess most days. But I'm working on it. Truly I am.

Oftentimes you can find me alternating between belting out my favorite praise songs and eating all of my feelings with a jar of Nutella.

I'm learning, though, that we ought to do something great with whatever we've survived. To help someone else find their way out of the woods.

235

There's an immeasurable purpose for why we are all here on earth at this appointed time.

There's a reason you made it to the other side of whatever brokenness you've held—or are perhaps still fighting to survive.

There's a grit and an authority that come with our experiences. An open door to speak where you otherwise couldn't. To join a club you never would have understood before. And to bring hope and understanding to someone who felt like they were the only one before they met you.

God has overwhelmingly good things in store for you and for those He will set free through your story.

A deeply fulfilling life is inside each one of us. Where we can live the kind of happy that fills us to the brim with passion and purpose. Where making our greatest contribution in life and following our callings trump merely waking up each day and planting two feet on the floor. Which sometimes, I admit, is a victory in itself. But they are still two different things.

Don't get me wrong. It's awful when a situation doesn't work out the way we've planned. Or when the very thing we love most is ripped away far too soon. It hurts when we have to adapt to plan B, or D, or even Z, for that matter.

But God Himself—He's the hope. Not the dreams, or the wishes, or the way we thought our life would turn out.

It's Him. Him alone.

We live in a culture that is searching endlessly for purpose and trying to be it all, do it all, and have it all. The funny thing about it is that as believers, we already have it all. In Him.

> LORD, you alone are my portion and my cup;
>   you make my lot secure.
> The boundary lines have fallen for me in pleasant places;
>   surely I have a delightful inheritance.
> I will praise the LORD, who counsels me;
>   even at night my heart instructs me.

I keep my eyes always on the LORD.
 With him at my right hand, I will not be shaken.

Therefore my heart is glad and my tongue rejoices;
  my body also will rest secure,
because you will not abandon me to the realm of the dead,
  nor will you let your faithful one see decay.
You make known to me the path of life;
  you will fill me with joy in your presence,
  with eternal pleasures at your right hand
          (Psalm 16:5-11).

He's the gift that makes getting up each day worth it and brings purpose to every single thing we do.

Things haven't panned out the way I thought they would, but amid the tears and the grief of what I thought my life would be like, I've discovered something even more incredible. The life *He* has for me. It may not be the way I thought it would be, but when I stop to look around, it's so much sweeter than the daydreams I scribbled on my notebooks in school.

Following Christ rarely looks the way we think it will. Maybe you've been fired from your dream job, or you've lost a loved one, or a person who said they'd always stay, didn't. You're not alone, friend. Just look at the lives of Noah, or Elijah, or David, or Moses, or Joseph. I don't think any of them would have voluntarily signed up for the life they lived. Yet they loved God, and they kept walking through what came at them. They held on to God, and He was faithful. And we have the history that we do because of their faith.

> If the enemy can get us to focus on all that we *don't* have, he will successfully deem us paralyzed to steward anything we *do* have.

As believers, we almost always find ourselves in the middle of experiences, situations, and lessons that we wouldn't have planned for ourselves. None of us really gets the life we thought we would, but if we surrender, we can learn to love the life God gives.

In a world where we are shown perfect homes, marriages, jobs, friendships, vacations, and families in spades, we can simultaneously feel inspired one minute and that our lives are completely inadequate the next. I think distraction and discontentment are two of Satan's most successful tools these days. If the enemy can get us to focus on all that we *don't* have, he will successfully deem us paralyzed to steward anything we *do* have.

Somewhere along the way we've got to pick up this faith of ours and live like we actually mean it. We've got to act like the Christ we say we believe. We need to lean in, build bridges, reach out when we need to, stay when it hurts, prune what needs pruning, and stand firm in what God is asking us to dig into.

We can't keep looking back at all that we've lost and expect to be able to move forward. We can't let the overwhelm of what we don't have oppress us into apathy.

We need to look another way. We need to start keeping a scorecard of all the good God has done, not just the grief we've walked through. We must make an intentional choice to remember all of the answered prayers, right decisions, miraculous protections, and seemingly random blessings that God has poured out on our lives.

If that feels hard, start writing them down. Make a list. That's what helped me turn the corner in my own life. I promise the first ones to write out are the hardest. But I've found that once I start recognizing the good, and being thankful for the blessings, it turns my eyes to look for the good, and it becomes easier and easier to find the nuggets of gold in our rocky lives.

It's amazing how different life looks when I lift up my head. When I put on new lenses and choose the hope that lives inside of me, through Him, every day. When I count gifts and not mistakes. And soak in the complex simplicity of having a Savior in the first place.

And now that I remember the Hope I have access to, I'm calling on the Source to bring back the joy too. And I know He will, because I'm finally trusting in Him: the God of hope.

Today I sit thankful for the sun on my back, knowing it is a rich gift. Thankful for laughter. For a family that stays. For you, dear reader, that you've stuck with me this far. For more blessings than I can possibly count.

For hope.

My heart is overflowing, and I'm even thankful for thankfulness. And the gift of perspective it brings.

I realized I had been hoping in the wrong things for far too long. I had been hoping in my circumstances changing, when really, the Hope I needed all along has lived inside me since the day I invited Him in.

And that, right there, is where this unexplainable peace is coming from.

I guess it is true what they say…we do find what we have eyes to see.

And I've found that *having it all* isn't all that mysterious. Because we have the gift of Christ, who brought us life to the fullest.

We just have to choose intentionally, to grab hold, actually believe it, and keep walking and acting as though we do.

And God is able to bless you abundantly, so that in all things at all times, having all that you need, you will abound in every good work.

2 CORINTHIANS 9:8

About the Author

Karen Stott is a visionary, entrepreneur, and fireman's wife who found her heartbeat while encouraging women that the good stuff is worth fighting for. She is the creator of Adventures with Archer and Intentional Home; and she is the founder of Haven Hill Ministries, which exists to bring hope, healing, and purpose to the world. Karen and her husband, Isaac, spend their days loving, adventuring, and forgiving with their three kids in the Oregon hills. Visit her at www.anintentionalhome.com.

To learn more about Karen,
visit our website at www.harvesthousepublishers.com.